FOR LOVE
OF THE
GAME

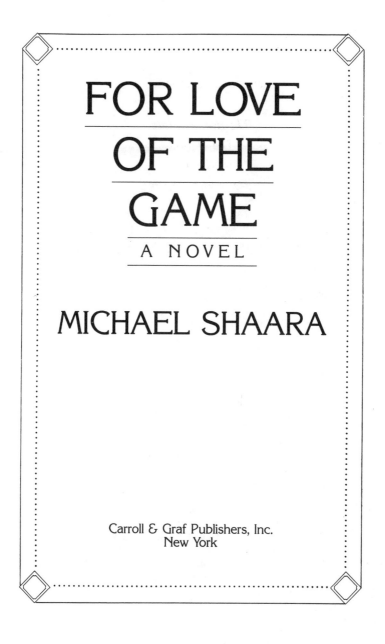

FOR LOVE
OF THE
GAME

A NOVEL

MICHAEL SHAARA

Carroll & Graf Publishers, Inc.
New York

First Carroll & Graf edition 1991

Carroll & Graf Publishers, Inc.
260 Fifth Avenue
New York, NY 10001

ISBN 0-7867-0114-5

Manufactured in the United States of America
April 1994

"Clay lies still, but blood's a rover;
Breath's a ware that will not keep.
Up, lad: when the journey's over
There'll be time enough to sleep."

—A.E. HOUSMAN

THE
HOTEL

Chapel checked into the usual hotel just after dark. He was deeply in the mood for an elegant supper in that elegant town with that elegant girl, but she didn't come. He put some music on the cassette player he always carried with him in the suitcase and lay down to rest and dream and wait, listening to Brahms. She was often late. She sometimes took time to make herself look spectacular and he didn't mind that at all, no hurry, he could always stand hunger. Music ended. No phone call. He turned on the TV. Nothing much. He thought: hell, let's have dinner here. Comfy dinner. Cozy dessert. Warm warm warm. You pitch tomorrow anyway. So . . . so what? Chapel finally looked at his watch. More than half an hour. Unusual. Give her a buzz? No. Not Carol. Don't prod Carol. Not yet. Not that girl. Patience, lad, patience. He lay back on the bed and shifted to an old cassette of Neil Diamond—"I am, I said, to no one there, and no one heard at all, not even a chair. . . ." Carol did not come.

By nine o'clock he knew something had gone wrong. Never this late. She would have called. In four years—it was that long! Amazing!—she was sometimes more than a half hour late and then always apologized and damn near went down on her knees—oh, yes, how well do I remember. She got down on her knees once and kissed me from that position, and we laughed, and loved, and laughed all that night. Where the hell? Something wrong. Must call. No. Don't call office. Chapel called her home phone number. Let it ring. No answer. Well. She got sent off somewhere. She'll try to call, I know. He called the desk.

"Yessir, Mr. Chapel, how you doin'?"

"I'm doin' fine. Listen, I'm waiting for a call from a woman named Grey, Carol Grey. If it comes, make sure you put that one through. Carol Grey. Got it?"

It was standard down there for them to keep people away from him, especially as the hours got late, and the phone in his room rarely rang, so he wanted there to be no mistake about Carol.

"Gotcha. Carol Grey. Will do. Hey, Mr. Chapel, you pitchin' tomorra?"

"Yep. Far as I know."

"Hey, man, you put em *down*. Okay? I ain't no fan of them guys. They snotnoses, and thassafack. Good luck to ya. Well, sir, good night now, sir. I got your lady's name. Carol Grey. Will put her right on through, soon as she calls. Luck, Mr. Chapel."

Chapel hung up and lay down and watched television.

Christ.

Think she got hurt?

In this damn town they get mugged. But . . .

she's been here long enough to take care of herself. Knows what she's doin'. Girl takes care of herself. Great faith in—not girl. *Woman.* She's aware of *that.* She is . . . thirty-four. Birthday? Yes. Remember? Last month, August—she's a Leo, her regal royal highness—boy, did we celebrate. But—she got very drunk. Unusual now for that girl. Always could hold the stuff. He saw the image clearly in his mind for one long moment: that long tall blonde lovely girl kneeling on the bed in a half slip, hair wildly flowing across her face, tangled, eyes glazed, one arm waving vaguely, giving the queen's speech, and then she fell forward in such a way as to hurt herself if he hadn't caught her. She passed out that night. Yep. She did. He remembered tenderly fondly drunkenly tucking her in and the way she reached out for him with both arms and hugged him for one long silent moment, so tightly he had to gasp, and then she faded away, and he sat there for a long time in the dark, with the music, hoping she'd be okay and wouldn't get sick, she never had before, and watching the light flow in from the window across that splendid face—but there was sadness on that face, and she dreamed a bad dream—what the hell about?—groaned, tossed. That night he thought it was only too much drinking. That was birthday number . . . thirty-four. So. Some birthdays are special. Maybe to her that night there was something . . . she couldn't talk about. She doesn't talk about sad things. But sad birthdays? Chapel was thirty-seven. He sat there sinking into a chair, watching a TV series of lovely girls: *Charley's Angels.* . . . What was the birthday that mattered to *you?* From . . . twenty-nine to thirty. Oh, well. From boy to man. In one whole day.

Where the hell is she?

She didn't get hurt in a car. Hell, doesn't even drive in this town. But could some dumb bastard have hit her cab, some drunken bastard? Possible. In this town they drive like . . . blink. Let that go. Chapel's parents had died in a car wreck years ago. Memories of some things . . . get in the way. Erase that. Clear the mechanism . . . go on waiting. No phone call. Back to Brahms. Academic Festival Overture. Didn't fit. He cut to silence. Food? Room service? No. Don't just sit here. He called the desk, told them he'd be down in the restaurant if Carol called. He put on a jacket, knotted a rare tie, went down and had something. They knew where to seat him and he was off by himself, but the waiter knew him, a man he called Soho, with an English accent which was not fake, and the waiter wanted to know if he was going to pitch tomorrow.

He went back up to his room and waited, but Carol didn't come. He was pitching the next day; there were only two days left in the season and two games left and it was his last outing and then he was free. Last time out so . . . rest. But do you rest . . . when she doesn't come. Why didn't she come? She'll tell you tomorrow. Very good sensible decent kind honest patient gentle reason. So let it go and think of something sober and industrious and the end of the season and going to ski in New Zealand in the winter and . . . rest. Have often stayed up all night before a game. Pride yourself on that. So did the Babe. Right? Right-ho. So. He listened to music but felt wounded doing that, alone, and laughed at himself and went back to TV, and what came in on the late show was *Arsenic and Old Lace*. That was a very funny movie coming back from his childhood and he really began to watch, began to laugh. Cary Grant was, ah, magnificent, and then that deathless line: "Insanity runs in the family. It practically *gallops.*" He loved that all over again—wish she was here to share the funny moments of this one, this was special, one of the great ones, but—nobody there. She would have really enjoyed this . . . wouldn't she? Ole Carol? Now *that* girl has a sense of humor. She's first of all a doll, a natural-born doll, she has a marvelous figure, and she . . . is as funny a girl as I've ever known. Right. That time, oh my God, the time she showed up wearing that wig to the hotel, speaking with a magnificent French accent: "*Je voudrais* something something. *Mais oui?* May we? *Enchanté,* mess you, you mess you. *Enchanté,* the moment he entered her. First time he ever broke up laughing while trying to make love to a lovely girl. That night . . . was a spectacular night. She certainly never cried. Never have seen her cry. Could she be crying tonight? Christ, is she all right? Call hospitals?

Dope.

Too many hospitals in this town.

She could have called.

If she could.

Couldn't.

Run off with another . . . chap.

Possible.

Definitely possible.

Carol?

Would she do that?

Not without . . . telling you.

Well, then. What do you think?

She's hurt.

Christ.

Nothing to do now.

Pitch tomorrow.

He turned off the TV and the music and lay for a long while in the dark. Season ends. We go back to New Zealand, like we did last year. He lay remembering skiing in the white New Zealand snow with Carol, down a glacier once, and the blue lake at Queenstown, and the mountains to the west on the South Island, over where they mined jade rock, and the lakes, the hills, as beautiful a place as there was on this earth. He went back to music, something very soft, and fell asleep. It was at that time past five in the morning.

Phone rang. Chapel groped, gathered.

"Hey there, Mr. Chapel. Wake-up call. Nine-thirty, sir."

"Um. Right. Thanks."

"One thing, Mr. Chapel. You remember that little bucket of baseballs you said you'd autograph? How 'bout that? They done? I can have Louie pick 'em up when he brings the coffee."

"Oh. Oh, fine. Okay."

"Right. Then he'll be up in a few minutes."

"Check."

"Hey, Mr. Chapel, you pitchin' today?"

"Ah. Think so."

"Shucks. Now, please don't be hard on those boys, Mr. Chapel. They *need* this one. You know. Listen, today, why don't you just take a good rest. You sure deserve it."

"Well."

"Sorry. But I'm behind my boys. Well, sir, have a good day."

Chapel hung up, stared across the nightstand at the small bucket of fresh new white baseballs. She never called. Got to sign those. Gee. I don't sign well. Never can read the blinkin' name. Why didn't she call? He reached out for the baseballs, saw underneath the bucket a layer of pictures he'd taken in New Zealand last year and had blown up, Carol on skis—they were together for Gus to see. Gus wants to go to New Zealand. We had plans. Boy oh boy. Calmly. " 'Tis the early morning," as Mom used to put it. Coffee and calm. But why in hell . . . clear the mechanism.

Chapel stood, searched round for a pen, drank a glass of cold water, then sat down on the big chair and started signing the baseballs, about twenty of them, for a club of injured kids.

His name was William Edward Chapel, but he signed as he was known: Billy Chapel. He been pitching in the major leagues for one team only, had never changed teams in seventeen years. That was very unusual in the major leagues now, but it had not been when he first came up to make his debut at the age of twenty, and he had never wanted to go anywhere else.

He was considered by most experts to have been one of the great pitchers in baseball history; his records were already ranked with those of Koufax and Feller and Spahn and Christy Mathewson, and though he was now thirty-seven years old and pitching these days with a last-place team which had gone far downhill in the past few years and so had not at all helped his numbers in the record books, he had begun to be regarded, at the age of thirty-seven, as one of the grand old men of baseball and he knew that well. He loved the game. He had loved it naturally all his life, since his first game as a small boy. He was a tall man, slim, long-armed, dark-haired, with gray hair at the temples, and his face had become widely known across the country because of a series of commercials he'd done on television and wished he hadn't done, and he had dark eyes, a sharp, pointed nose, and the thing about his face that always seemed to radiate when he was out on the mound was that he had the eyes of a winner. He looked at you and smiled. And won. He did not do much talking to anybody. He liked all kinds of music and all sorts of reading and travel, and he didn't argue with umpires or get into fights. He was a wandering man who had loved airplanes along with baseball and who had never married, although the next thing he had always loved, after the game, and flying, had always been women. He had known many beautiful girls. He had never been in love with one and had never even used the word. He was in many ways still very young in the mind and he was aware of that. Billy Boy, Billy Boy, you'll have to grow up someday. He would. He had been . . . attached to that one woman, Carol Grey, the delightful blonde, for four years, and it was a long time now that he had taken no other woman but her anywhere. She had been married once —badly; the scars there were still rather obvious and she did not want any more of *that*. She did not want children. If she ever married again it would be to a rich and older man who tired easily and rested a lot and left her alone in a lovely house. She worked in this town for a publisher—now a full-scale editor with a growing reputation—but she traveled often to see him during the season and he came to be with or near her when the season was done, although his home base was the high country out in Colorado, and they had had four very good years, years which admittedly confusingly got better and better. Very well educated, well read, lovely girl with great social grace, spending most of her spare time with a big kid baseball player. They smiled when they saw each other. Had from the beginning. Never anything complex or serious. She came to him to relax and laugh and giggle and play games, and ski and fly airplanes and never fight. Never once. Over anything at all. Disagree: yes. Tactfully, quietly. Over in a moment. Knew little of the mountains, and he'd taken her . . . many places. Taught her to ski. In two weeks they were scheduled to be heading for New Zealand. And . . . she didn't show.

Chapel signed the last baseball. Looked at his watch. Almost ten. She'd be in her office. If. . . . He knew the number. Dialed.

So long to answer. Always. Ring ring ring. Then, at last:

"Hell-llo. Rogers and Stein Publishing. Can I help you?"

"Like to speak to Miss Grey, please. Carol Grey. Is she in?"

"Just a moment." Pause. "Oh, hey, is this Mr. Chapel? Billy Chapel? Is that whom I'm speaking to?"

"Right. It's me. Is Carol there?"

"Well, *hello*, Mr. Chapel. How you doin'? Nice to hear from you. Ah. Just a minute. One minute. What? No. Oh. Mr. Chapel, sorry, but she's not in her office. They don't know where she is. I'll have her paged." Pause. "Well now, are you pitchin' today, Mr. Chapel?"

"Guess so." Waiting.

"Golly, Mr. C.—you take it easy today on our fellas, you hear? Our boys need that game today, and *your* fellas don't. Isn't that so? Your team is *last*, so it sure don't matter to you, but I tell you, here around this office, the way people are excited. . . . Oh. I see. Ah, Carol's gone out. She'll be back in a bit, but nobody knows when. Maybe not this morning. Well. Any message you'd like to leave?"

Pause. She must be . . . okay. Unhurt. Just there. He said: "No message." Pause. "Just . . . tell her I called."

"I'll sure do that. Gee, I'm sorry about that ballgame stuff. But I have to root for my team, you understand that. You, of all people. I mean, I hope *you* don't lose, 'cause I sure think the world of you, I mean, who

doesn't? But I hope your team loses. Well. Nice to talk
to you."

Chapel put down the phone.

Strange cold morning. Odd weather we're having.

She's gone to work. So. Health . . . no problem.
Well. Something happened last night . . . with the
family. Bad news. Don't jump up and down, Billy.
Never had a problem with that girl. Now finally a
problem. So all right. Calmly. Maybe you can help.
Maybe she'll need you. Patience, Billy Boy.

Knock on the door. Chapel pivoted: the door, un-
locked, swung slightly open, the big round bearded
face of Gus Osinski, the catcher, peeked round the
bend.

"Hey, man, is she decent?" Gus squinted round,
searching for Carol, assumed she was in the bathroom.
"I come in?"

He came into the room, a mass of pictures and
brochures tucked against his great chest. He plopped
them on the bed. No one but Gus would have opened
the door at this time of the morning. He was Chapel's
closest friend. Chapel's team changed every year, none
but Chapel had stayed for long, and Gus had only been
around for about four years, yet of all the catchers
Chapel had known, he worked best with Gus. A plan
had been building to get together after the season and
head for New Zealand, where Gus had never been,
and Chapel had supplied Gus with a mass of informa-
tion. The big man patted a mound of pictures, gave
that massive grin.

"Man, these kept me up half the night. I showed

'em to Bobbie and I tell you, she's hooked. When do we go? Set the date. Glaciers, for Chrissake. I never seen a glacier. Whole damn frozen river. You know I don't ski? I don't. Not me. Christ, I'd be the biggest snowball since—but Bobbie can ski. She has two weeks easy, maybe three, from the airline, so set the date. It's spring there already, right? Here . . . two days left in September. What time is that in New Zealand? September, October. How do you work that out?"

"Figure the opposite," Chapel said.

"Which?"

"Well. September comes like March. October same as April. Then November is May, and so on. Their summer is our winter. Exact opposite. January to them is . . . July."

Gus had his mouth open, delighted, figuring. But he had looked at the bed and then was looking at it again and he saw that the bed was crumpled but the pillow was still under the blanket and the bed did not look slept in. Chapel had lain on it during the night but had not undressed. Gus looked round for Carol. No sign. He said: "What . . . ah . . . is she here?"

"Nope."

"Oh, boy. What happened?"

"She didn't show."

"Why not?"

"I don't know."

"A fight or somethin'?"

"I don't know."

"She just . . . didn't come last night? Well . . . didn't she call?"

"Nope." Chapel stood up, rubbed his beard. "Need a shave."

"Well, hell, man, is she okay?"

"Yep. I just called her office. Didn't talk to her. But . . . they said she came in."

"Ah," Gus said. Then he said, with deep sudden gloom: "Ah, shit."

Chapel looked down at the pictures near the cassette: that blond girl on skis. He picked up a cassette: Neil Diamond again, put it on automatically, punched the button. He said: "I don't know anything yet. I don't understand . . . not like her. Maybe it's just . . . something got in the way. She'll call later and tell me."

"Right. Christ, I hope so." Pause. "You and that woman . . . well. But what about our plan? Got to hold her to that, the trip to New Zealand—hey, there's this thing I want to ask you about marriage. Over there. I mean, how about the hotels over there if you check in with the lady who is not married to you? How do they feel about that? I've heard there are some places a little . . . behind the times. Especially them Catholic places. They tell me—hell, you know, I never been overseas—they tell me, a lot of guys, that if you pick up any broad and try to take her back to your room a lot of hotels won't let her in and I don't want any of that stuff, certainly not with Bobbie. My God, *Bobbie.*"

"You shouldn't have any problem. Not if you check in together. Not that I know of. I never had any. Bringing a girl *in*, I don't know about that. . . ."

Another Diamond song played.

Gus: "But her passport won't have a married name."

Chapel: "So if they ask, you got the passport before the marriage, and never did change it. But nobody ever asked us."

"Good. Great. Takes a load off my mind." Pause. "Man, have you been to sleep?"

"Forty winks."

Gus was watching him with concern. "I never been to a *real* foreign country before. Except parts of Canada. Hee. Hey. They all speak English in New Zealand, right? I mean, do they get sticky with another language, like in Canada?"

"No. They're kind of . . . Scotchmen. No problem."

"Good. The French and me, we don't see eye to eye."

Knock on the door. Again open immediately: the tall, lean bellhop whom Chapel had known for years, a cheerful black man named Louie, carrying the usual coffee and rolls and jelly, a broad grin, handsome features in a gleaming face.

"*Good* mornin', Mr. Chapel. How you doin' this mornin', sir? You got them baseballs all signed? Ah, right. Thank you, sir. Them kids, I tell you, them kids'll all go through the *wall*. They all know you, they see you in them commercials. Hey. You pitchin' today? How about that? You goin' in there today?"

"Think so." Chapel searched for the tip. The bell-hop was pouring the coffee. Two cups—he'd brought the extra for Gus. He stood up, that enormous grin growing wider. He cocked his arm like a warrior about to hurl a spear. "Well, I hope you blow 'em away. Zoom!" He whirled his arm and fired: strike. "Ha!" He flexed his arm, wrung it out, massaged the muscle with the other hand, like an old and mighty pro. He moved with natural grace—ex-dancer? He was saying: "I live in this town, but that ain't *my* team. Motherless bastards. All you gotta do is work for 'em *once*, and, man, the things I could tell ya. . . ." He picked up the baseball bucket. " 'Preciate it, Mr. Chapel, 'preciate it. I know the kids that'll . . . well. Good luck, sir. Hope you go out there today and"—he gave a cheery, evil grin—"and *dust* 'em off, Mr. Chapel. Just dust 'em off." He departed.

"His own hometown." Gus was slightly wounded. "Well, I betcha he just doesn't come from here."

The Neil Diamond song was beginning to annoy Chapel, and that was unusual: he turned the thing off, stood there, picked up another: old stuff, folk songs, Burl Ives, kept the hands moving, put on another cassette.

Gus: "Got to tell you this, Chappie, I get cold up *here* in the winter, so, if you don't mind, I'd just as soon—"

The phone rang.

Carol?

But Gus was near: picked it up.

"Yeah. Right. Who? Well. Okay. Here." He handed the phone to Chapel. "Manager at the desk."

Chapel took the thing, put it to the ear. The voice was one of the head men downstairs whose name Chapel did not know. The man was excited.

"Mr. Chapel. Ah, yes. Sorry to disturb you, sir, normally wouldn't do that kind of thing at all, but, ah, there's a gentleman down here who wishes to see you, sir, in person, and, well, sir, the gentleman is rather, ah, well, he's that television personality, sportscaster, whatever the word is, well, *everybody* knows Ross. I mean, it's that fella from NBC, D.B. Ross. You're, well, familiar, of course. If you don't mind, he, ah, tells me that he *must* speak to you as soon as possible, that the matter is, ah, urgent, and that he prefers to do it privately, and not on the telephone. Can he come up?"

After a moment Chapel said: "Is he alone?"

"Alone? Oh. Oh, yes, sir."

"Well. Okay."

"Fine! Thank you, sir. He'll be right up."

News? Something had happened. Clutch in the chest: pressure, warning. No. Don't think. He drank the coffee.

Gus: "Dooby Ross. Jeez. I wonder. . . ."

Chapel: "I need a shave."

Gus: "I'd watch this bird. Chappie, take care. This guy is what they call a 'showboat.' Want me to move out? Leave you alone?"

"Hell, no."

"Shit. This guy, in some ways, is worse than Cosell. Ah. I was hopin' it was Carol. Hey. Now, Billy?"

"Yep."

"Want you to know, before somebody comes. I hope you fix that up. I think a lot of her. And if you don't fix it up—Christ, how long have you known that girl? Years and years. You two . . . went good together. You looked good together. Matching pair. I mean, with that girl, you *laugh*. So I really hope—for your sake—Jesus. Is it *marriage?* Is that the point? Is it time for . . . time to be practical? Ha? What you think?"

Chapel said nothing. Songs often went through his mind, were singing in the back of the brain while he worked, and that one song was repeating itself there now as he stood by the pictures:

Are you goin' away, with no word of farewell?
Will there be not a trace left behind?
Well, I could have loved you better
Didn't mean to be unkind
As you know
That was the last thing on my mind . . .

Knock on the door. This time it didn't open. Chapel: here he comes. To Gus he nodded. Gus opened the door: Dooby Ross.

He was famous among television people, had been a sportscaster going back a long ways, back almost to the days of Red Barber, Mel Allen. He was a round, bald man with a flaxen mustache which was his "trademark," that old-fashioned barber's mustache. He had a small, round nose, sharp black eyes, a derby he held in his hand. Smartly dressed: a silvery tie, flicker of something diamondlike in the center, a light gray coat. He came into the room, stopped, making an entrance, gazed across the room at Chapel, a brief glance at Gus, then a slight bow.

"Billy Chapel. My pleasure to see you."

Chapel nodded.

"What's on your mind?"

The dark eyes were watching, calculating. Chapel knew: he brings bad news. A trade. . . .

Ross, the showman, paused there for a long moment, took a deep breath. Then he said slowly, clearly: "There is some news that will break in a few days. It's being held back now by the people who know about it, but I found out about it myself last night. I learned from a . . . friend. Billy, it's about you." Pause. "The news shook me up. First thing I thought of was: Billy should know. I owe it to you. After all these years. I owe it to you."

Chapel, softly: "You don't owe me anything."

Ross let that pass. He was making his presentation. He folded his arms behind him. "They made the deal in quiet. Sometime last week. They were going to hold it back until the season was over and not let you know till then. That's only—a few days off. But they figured it was better not to break the news now. But when they let it loose, Billy, they won't tell you first.

Just as they do so often with . . . Willie Mays, fellas like that. The big boys they—can't face. So. You'll hear it on the news or read it in the paper, and that's the first they expect you to know."

Chapel knew: traded. It was a cold blossom blooming in the chest.

Ross: "When I found out about it, last night, first thing I thought was this: he should know. Billy should know. Right now. Let him find it out alone. Don't let them . . . mob the guy with questions."

"Trade," Chapel said.

Ross, no word necessary, nodded.

Long moment of silence.

Chapel looked at Gus. Gus had turned away. Chapel said, after a while: "Traded. Who to?"

Ross: "Don't yet know. Not yet. I'm workin' on it. All I know is, a team out on the West Coast. I got that far. From a girl that . . . hell. That's not the point. Here's the point, Billy. They can get a lot of money out of you right now and they know it, and the word is that you don't have much more time as a starting pitcher anymore. You're thirty-seven. They can make big money if they move now. There are a few teams who think that with you in their bullpen they can go to the World Series. And they know how you feel, Billy—" He bared his teeth, gave the look of smelling something sick. "Oh, sure, they know that all right. But dammit, Billy, you played the honorable man all the way. You never came out of the goddam eighteenth century. Christ, Billy, you never made any real legal deal. They've got you by the balls, *by the living balls,* and they know that, I know that, goddammit, you know that. You must know that. You just never thought—while the Old Man was around. But Billy, he's gone now. And the little men are in there now. And, Billy Boy, you're gone now, too. That's the goddam miserable shiteating truth. You won't be with the Hawks next year. Billy, it's done. And there's nothin' you can do."

Chapel turned, saw a chair; sat.

Music from the cassette: "The pony run he jump he pitch . . . he threw my master in the ditch. . . ."

Chapel cut it.

Stillness.

Empty inside. Nothing there. Head gone empty.

Song was: "The Blue Tail Fly."

He heard Gus swear. Chapel looked up vacantly, smiled, seeing nothing. Remembered the Old Man, smoking a big fat brown smoky cigar: "Billy, goddammit, one of these days, goddammit, you got to grow up and play for *money*, like they all do. All them little bastards."

Chapel nodded. But . . . I never did.

And now . . . seventeen years with one team. Signed . . . on the front porch with the Old Man and Pop all those years ago . . . vision blurred. Ah, but the Old Man loved the game, and Pop loved the game, and I loved it so . . . and every year, the Old Man did the best he could . . . in the office, the round, frowning face: "Billy, kid, this is the best I can do. But you are the best no matter what I do. But I can't do better. But if this *bothers you*, Billy, if it ain't enough, you tell me, and I'll try, so help me, I'll borrow someplace. Billy, what do you want?"

The Old Man is gone.

What do you want?

Knew this day would come.

Did you?

Yep. But. Well.

It's come.

Yep.

Chapel had seen this coming, knew it was coming, and had planned nothing, nothing at all.

Ross was watching. No questions. He turned to Gus, eyed, calculated.

"You Gus Osinski, right? The catcher?"

"Yep."

"You're hitting, ah." Ross put a finger to his nose, a famous position of mind packed with filed numbers. "You're hitting right now . . . 206. Am I right?"

Gus grunted. "Close enough."

Ross smiled, blinked, his mind moving along, rounding bends, from Gus to Billy and back. Ross said: "You know the point, Gus. They'll say to the home fans he's over the hill. Look at the record this last year. . . ."

"Look at the club behind him. Look at *that* batting average. That bunch can't hit as good as *me.*"

"I know. But the records, the numbers . . . and his *name.* Seventeen years with the same club. The novelty of it. To have Billy Chapel on the mound for . . . *them,* whoever the hell they are, maybe LA, maybe the Giants. They'll pack 'em in out there for a while, just to see him, root for him. Even if only a few innings at a time. . . . Even if only in relief. . . ."

"Billy? In relief? Ha. Not him. Never. *Never.*"

"He won't go. You don't think so." Ross turned back to Chapel, Billy sat there, no expression at all, drinking coffee. Ross came forward, stood in front of him. His speech was faster now, more intense: he was getting to the point.

"Billy, I came here because I thought I owed it to you. Now, I *do*"— he put out both hands—"I know that in ways you never will. So. I thought I could let you know this thing in private, away from the crowd, the way they've done it so often. I didn't want to see you, Billy, with them asking all those questions in public. So." Pause. "I came up as fast as I could." Pause. "And now you know the facts. You know what they want to do. But, Billy . . . I have a *hunch.*" He cocked a finger, like a man about to pull the trigger on an invisible gun. He smiled a strange, soft smile. "Billy Boy, Chappie, you're the best I ever saw. I don't say this for publicity. No cameras watching. But I want you to know what I think. After seventeen years . . . Billy, you're the best." Pause. He had said something that to him was very important and very unusual. Then his face recovered, and there came back that crafty natural grin. "So. You are the best. And when a man like you is truly the best and knows it, like Ted Williams knew it, and DiMaggio, and a few of the golden boys, there comes that special *pride.*" Pause. Smile. "I think I've got you figured, Billy, but . . . who knows? Still . . . I've got this guess. You have been traded to another team after seventeen years with the Hawks . . . one place, one home, and now they've let you go; no, they've thrown you away. They do that to all the big boys sooner or later. Hell, they did it to Babe Ruth, to make money, and he went, and Willie Mays, and Maury Wills. And most of them . . . they go on playing. But, Billy"—he leaned forward now, face coming in closer to Billy's face, eyes there boring into Billy's eyes—"with you, Billy, I think it could be different. Some of the guys didn't go. There were guys like Williams, and Joltin' Joe. They had the pride. When they were done, *they were done.* Isn't that so? You know it like I do, yes you do, Billy, you know the pride. When they were done, when there was the first flaw, when the leg didn't quite work anymore for Joe or Williams wasn't exactly the best anymore, as soon as the hints were there, even the *hints,* they would play no more. They were done. They would take no trade. Willie Mays . . . Willie, I saw him out there one day, drop a fly ball. Tears in his eyes. But he had to go on. Some guys love it that way, the pride doesn't matter. Some guys, just the money. But you, Billy . . . well. Will you tell me? Are you done? Or will you go on to another team? What'll it be?"

Chapel sat for a long moment in a silent room without any motion. Ross couldn't wait. He said: "I came to you with the news, to break it to you as a favor."

Chapel nodded, said nothing.

"Now, Billy, will you do this for me, will you tell me what you're going to do? Can you tell me now?

Because Billy, now that you know, I'll tell you this: I've got a hunch. A big hunch. It will make big good news. Billy, I don't think you'll go. I think you're done." Pause. Silence. "Am I right?"

Chapel didn't want to sit anymore, didn't want to talk. He stood up rubbing his face. He said: "Shave, I think. Excuse me."

He walked away. Ross said nothing. Chapel went into the bathroom and closed the door. He felt pain and darkness for the first time. Hit very hard. He went mechanically to the mirror and looked into it and did not see himself as he began to soap his face. He thought no words. For a moment he saw the happy face of his father, Pops, pounding a hand in the catcher's mitt they had practiced with when Billy was a pup, and he *heard* Pop's voice: "Come on, Billy! Throw hard now, Billy Boy!" He began slowly to shave. Softly, the old folk song: "Oh where have you been, Billy Boy, Billy Boy? Oh where have you been, charming Billy?"

First thought: I guess he's right.

Chapel stopped shaving.

Time to go home.

Play no more?

At all, at all?

"What, never? Thou'll come no more, never?"

This . . . is a hell of a day.

He tried to clear the mind but it wouldn't clear, wouldn't think. He finished shaving, stood there by the door, not wanting to go back in to talk to Ross. One more moment. He heard Ross's voice:

". . . for four years with that man, right? Yes, I know, you've been traded yourself, what, three times? Not the same thing for you, is it? But him? Listen, you've been catching Chapel for four years. You know him like nobody else. What do you think? Go ahead, give it straight. You think he's over the hill?"

Gus's voice, sudden and harsh:

"Horseshit! Ole Chappie? Over the hill? Pure horseshit! Listen, ace, you try and catch him yourself, first few innings. Hail Mary. Give him to anybody. Then stand back. He is . . . he is still the *fastest* I ever saw, and along with that the control. My God, near perfect. He does it all. Shit, he can thread needles with bullets. With any kind of team at all . . . hell, he still holds half the records. Christ, you know that. And he's thirty-seven. So what? Only problem is he . . . he just doesn't last as long as he used to. He tires earlier. A little like Ole Bobby Feller. *He* wasn't before your time, you remember him. Christ, if baseball was a game only lasted six innings nobody ever would have beaten that guy. But he tired . . . a little too soon. And Billy's now that way. In the beginning, nobody hits him. Those first few innings, God Almighty . . . he was always the best. He's *still* the best. Hell. Ask anybody. Anybody who has to go up against him."

Pause.

Ross said: "So. Agreed. But. What do you think he'll do?"

"Ah. I don't know."

"You think he'll go play on the Coast because he

loves the game? Because he never really played for the money?"

"Don't know."

"What would you do?"

"Me? Why the hell ask me?"

"What would you do?"

"I been traded . . . enough. Makes no more difference to me. To a lot of guys. So. I'd go. Just to play some more."

"Yes. And so would almost everybody. But Billy. . . ."

Chapel opened the door, came out into the room.

Ross: "Well, Billy?"

Chapel shook his head.

Ross: "Billy Boy, Billy Boy, how can you quit?"

Chapel looked round for his jacket. Go for a walk. Ole buddy.

Ross: "What about you pitchin' . . . today?"

Chapel stopped.

Ross: "They have you scheduled for today. Nobody's supposed to know. But . . . what do you do now?"

Chapel saw the jacket, picked it up.

The phone rang. Gus was there, lifted it quickly.

"Hello hello. Listen. . . . What? Jesus." He looked wide-eyed at Chapel. "Hey, man. It's Carol." Pause. "What do I do?"

Chapel went for the phone, hand extended. He said: "Hello?"

Soft, breathy voice: "Billy?"

"Yep."

"This is me."

Carol. Where?

"Hi," Chapel said.

"I'm over in the park. Cross the way."

"Uh-huh."

"Billy?"

"Yep."

"I'm over by the fountain. I've been there looking up at your window."

Pause. Ross was tapping fingers on top of the couch; Gus was signaling him to shut up, finger at the lips.

Carol: "You know the fountain. The one you can . . . almost see me from your window."

"Oh, yeah. I know."

"Well. I . . . didn't want to come up there this morning. I'm sorry. Last night was . . . bad. Well. I just quit my job. I'm leaving town. But before I go . . . would you talk to me for a minute? Would you come down here and talk to me? The crowd over there . . . Would you do that? Please?"

"Oh, sure," Chapel said.

"You will? Oh . . . thank you. I'll . . . when will you be here? I can wait."

Chapel: "Be right there. A few minutes."

He put down the phone. Dazzled brain. Glad she called. Got to talk. What to wear? Got the jacket. Fine.

Ross was saying: "Billy, there's not a hell of a lot of time. What are you gonna do?"

Chapel: "I'm goin' down to the park."

Ross: "Are you gonna pitch today?"

Gus: "Carol. Good thing, buddy. Hope it works."

Knock on the door: Chapel opened it: the blue-clad stewardess: Bobbie, Gus's girl. Dark-haired, slim, trim. She gave Chapel a lovely smile.

"Hi there."

Chapel started out by her. Ross came, caught his shoulder.

"Billy, dammit, I need to know. There's just no time."

Chapel: "I'll let you know. But I've got to go. Maybe I'll see you at the ballpark. By that time, maybe. . . ."

But Ross hung on to him:

"Billy, I think you've got the pride. I don't think you'll go. Not anywhere. I think you're through, Billy. I think it's all over."

Chapel turned, looked at the round white face. Moment of silence. Then Chapel said: "You may be right."

"Can I print that?"

Chapel closed his eyes. Then he said: "Just a little while. I'll tell you . . . at the ballpark."

He pulled away, started down the hall.

Ross said: "Billy, I did you a favor. Don't you owe me?"

Chapel looked, paused, nodded. He said: "Soon as I can. I . . . appreciate it. But . . . well. See you."

He went away down the hall. The last he heard was the voice of Bobbie:

"Hey. Did you find out? Do I have to tell everybody we're married?"

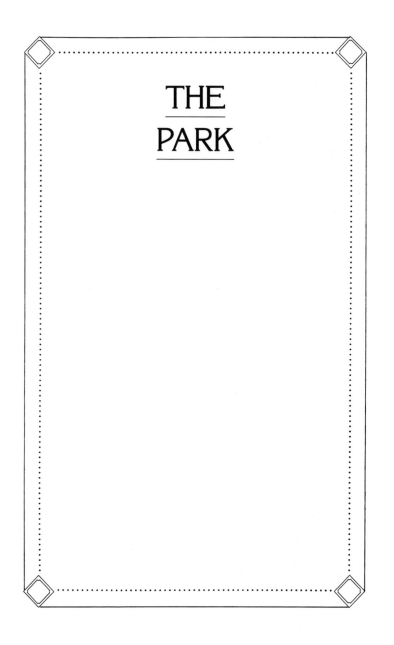

THE
PARK

There had been rain that morning, much rain; there were pools on the grass and a low gray misty sky, and Chapel thought: no ball game today? Solve everything. Thanks, Boss. Pack up tonight. Off to Colorado. Home.

As he came out of the hotel the doorman saw him and bawled aloud: "Hey, Mr. Chapel! You pitchin' to-day? Jeez, I hope not." Heads turned to look his way, but he hopped on across the street and into the park and there were very few people there in the morning, a few joggers, and Chapel jogged himself toward the fountain where Carol was waiting, splashing his way through cold puddles. He was very glad she had called. He did not know who or what was waiting. Met her four years ago, almost to the day, at that party: flashes now in the mind's clear eye of that tall stately blonde on the far side of the room, one of the most beautiful things he had ever seen, lighted up the magic lantern —what poem was that?—and they were to kid about that sight across the room, the "crowded room," one night while watching *South Pacific* on the late movie: "Some enchanted evening, you will see a stran-gerrr, across a crrrrowded room. And somehow you know, you know even then—" And by God, it was true. She met what she called "the great one." Not long after that one all-star game where he struck out the side with the bases loaded in that one great inning which made him as much of a celebrity as he was ever to be, and so she met him knowing that. She had never known ballplayers. Not the type. She was an educated, beautiful woman in the publishing business who had traveled widely overseas and spoke several languages, and who had married a rich and mean bastard and managed to stay married in pain for almost ten years and was now divorced, at that party perfectly, permanently free, and more or less permanently drunk. But drunk or not, witty and educated and cocky or not, she was genuinely funny. She laughed him into the wall. He began to have good moments with her—he saw them in her eyes. He saw the eyes lighten, sparkle, beautiful, steamy eyes. He remembered suggesting that he go find the ex-husband and "lean on him." They went out and talked and went to bed and she passed out. He was odd in the morning, woke up looking down at her and feeling somewhat eerie. When she awoke she was—different. He was sorry she had been so mechanical. Lay there. So warm, so chilly. There was a new thing in her eyes that morning, someone sober looking at him who he did not understand at all. He remembered her sudden voice: "I won't do it again. I promise."

"Do what?"

"Fuck."

"What?"

"No. Too . . . casual. Sorry. Won't do that again."

"What, never?"

"Well." Smile began again. "Well, hardly ever."

Then she said: "Let's you and I . . . have fun. Together. I promise to be good to you. You're a good man, Chappie. You're just . . . a straight shooter. From the hip. Honest as a boy. I want to help you enjoy life a little. And you, me. You didn't really want me to fuck like that last night . . . because we didn't really know each other yet and it was too soon. I won't do that again. Please don't hold it against me."

He didn't hold it against her. They spent that day together. They sat and walked and talked all day and into the night. About marriage—hers—and death and God and school and baseball games and music. They went out that night and danced—*that* was a thing at which she was superb and he was not, and so she started to teach him, and she had real talent as a teacher, but he didn't as a dancer, and then he took her back to her apartment very late, almost dawn, and she did not even kiss him good night. She saluted him, as the lieutenant to the captain. Then she was gone. And from then on they saw each other every day he was in town . . . the ballplayer—she had never known an athlete of any kind at all and she was fascinated by the way he talked about it, living it with him. Then he left. And called when his team was back. And she was present in a splendid glow, and it was all very clear: they stopped seeing other people. She met him where he was playing in other towns: still didn't go to bed. Didn't talk about it. He played down in Atlanta and she came to stay with him for a week, and the right night came, and he felt the gigantic need and she opened, and it was in that enormously personal way different than it had ever been with anyone else, however much joy there had been in bed, where there had always been joy. From then on they bedded down as extraordinary adventurers, differently every time, in so many ways that for a short while it was a wild new game to two talented athletes, and then that passed and tenderness came, and they held each other wordlessly for a magic time, and never mentioned love. They were playing the greatest of games, but to Carol life was all a game, and she was going to play the damned thing from here on out and never again take anything seriously, the way poor Billy did too often when he lost, and so they did not use the word "love." She did not want to talk any more of normal life and marriage and she did not ever want to go back to "meditation," which had taught her nothing and made her very blue. She promised him: "Champ, we'll have a ball, as you fellas say, one way or the other. You'll never see me cry. Never. I'll cry to myself. And don't you cry to me. Billy, bless your head, you're more fun than any kid I've ever known. And you're such a lovely boy. A sweet sweet boy. So. Let's *do it*. Now. Chumley."

Four years. They would see each other three or four days at a time. Then nothing for perhaps a week, never longer than a month. In the winter he went home to Colorado for the Indian summer and she came out and then he came in, every month, and then they went one winter to New Zealand, but she stayed only three weeks because of her job, and then next year they went again, and it was better and then . . . this summer past . . . her birthday . . . she was weary. In the late innings. Hot summer. Work. Never ask questions. She'll tell you. But she was always *there* and he never told her troubles and sometimes she'd bitch a bit about the job, but never truly seriously in detail, never to lean on his shoulder and sob. They were light to each other whatever the darkness. But Billy Chapel needed no help against sadness. He took the death of his parents alone, no other way, no possible help. And that was true of the rest of it. He was playing toward the end with a very bad team that was there behind him and around him every day and was a weight, a growing weight, and he hated to lose but he had always been able to take that with faith that it was only temporary, that he'd win the next time, and they knew it, they knew it was only luck that beat him. He often lost now but he went right on with no less faith . . . and he did love the game, did love to play, he loved just to be out there throwing, planning, dreaming, thinking, and was cheered to rest and dream between the endless games, waiting, and then came that day, that night, when she did not come. All this was summing itself up in one long, wide picture flowing across his mind, reaching an end, a true end that morning, as he jogged down a winding puddled path toward the high-spouting fountain he saw at a distance—and there she was sitting, the golden blonde, the long and perfect, yes, *perfect* legs, sitting on a green bench dressed in a classic gray raincoat leaning forward staring into the fountain, both hands in her pockets, herself tucked inside the raincoat, huddled. Slight jolt to the eyes to see her. She looked up. He slowed, stopped, lifted the right hand, small salute.

"Howdy, ma'am."

"Hey."

She did not look into his face. She moved over a small way on the bench. He sat.

He said: "How you doin'?"

"I'm sorry."

"S'all right. I knew there was a good reason. I sure did miss you."

He saw a tear on the corner of her eye. She turned her face away.

She said: "I tried to make a telephone call. Couldn't. Dammit. When I tried to call, I'd start to cry." She pulled out a Kleenex from her purse, squeezed it, didn't put it to the eye. "I *hate* that. Goddammit. You never saw me cry. That was . . . the agreement. The deal."

"Why did you have to cry?"

"Ah." She shook her head. "I was drinking too much. Much too much. You know, Billy, honest, I sometimes drink too goddam much. I know, hard for you to believe, you know how . . . prissy I get . . . but, oh, hell. I was smashed. And when I get smashed, lately, you know? I get very sad." She glanced at him for the first time, then quickly away. She so rarely talked seriously about herself. He knew she was trying to break ground into something funny, but it wasn't going to work. She put up the Kleenex, covered her eyes. She said slowly: "Didn't want you to see me . . . *too* drunk. Really. It's unbecoming. There are things I say . . . Billy. . . ." Long pause. "We've had a good time, Billy."

Billy said: "Yep."

A couple came jogging by, round the fountain. On the sweatshirts: Harvard. Carol had settled a bit, composed, something firmer now in her voice, no longer that waver, but . . . there was something else. Billy watched.

Carol said: "Four years." Summing it up. As if: done. Truly done, over, finished. It hit him; he blinked. He said: "What's the matter?"

"I'm going home."

"Home?"

"I've quit the job."

"Oh."

"I did that this morning. I was going to tell you, but . . . ah. Well. You don't need me, Billy."

"I don't need you?" Amazed.

"Billy." She turned to look at his face, put out a hand, touched his shoulder. Her face had that deep, sweet softness. He realized she was saying good-bye.

"Billy Boy. I'm . . . back at my birthday. Do you remember? Thirty-four. I don't know what happened, what it was, that number doesn't mean anything, but suddenly, no, not even suddenly, it's been coming up out of the dark all this year, coming out of the old back of the aging head: time to move on, move on. Take

. . . the new path. Into old age. I was married all that
time and it was bad and I wanted something else and
got out, thank God, with you, sweet Billy, and the last
four years have been. . . ." Her voice began to fail;
she squeezed his shoulder. "It's been the best time,
Billy. I'll always . . . but now . . . things have
changed. Oh, God, how do I say this? Last spring I
began to look in the mirror. But it wasn't that. I began
to look out the window at the city, and then on the job
at all those faces . . . and finally, Billy," the tears
were swelling, "one day I just wanted to go *home*. Rest.
Start over. Somewhere else. I went back to see Mom.
You knew about that. You've never met Mom. She said
. . . come home for a while and just putter in the gar-
den. Just get away from that place for a while. So I
quit the job, but they'll let me come back if ever I . . .
but I won't. I'm going . . . I won't be back. I won't be
in this town anymore. And you . . . Billy . . . you
don't need me."

"Don't say that again," Chapel said. Then he said:
"There's also a man involved in this. Fella who needs
you. Are you thinkin' of . . . getting married?"

Carol looked into his eyes. Voice very quiet. She
said: "I haven't decided yet. Not yet."

"But there *is* a guy."

"Yes."

Chapel said nothing. No promises broken, no
word ever given. Free. Carol said: "I didn't hide anything, Billy. I didn't do anything with . . . him. But
he's a good, quiet man. Gentle. I don't love him. Understand that. Please, Billy? He's a good, quiet man

who seems to love me. Has from the beginning. Wants
to take care of me . . . 'forever.' He has a fine home
. . . we'd go overseas a lot. He's much older than you,
Billy. He first asked me early in the summer."

"You going to marry him."

"I don't know."

Chapel put his hand to his face, rubbed his nose.
"Handsome fella?"

"No."

"That's good." Chapel shrugged, blinked.
"Christ," he said. "This is my day."

"Billy?"

He looked up. She moved her hand down to his.
"There was nothing wrong you ever did. But, Billy
. . . time goes by. I saw this title of a book: *Childhood's
End.* I'm getting old all of a sudden, Billy. I don't know
why. I won't be fun anymore. When you go away
now. . . ."

"I'll be far away," Chapel said.

Another couple came jogging by. Coincidence.
This time: Yale.

Chapel said: "They never can trade you there.
Never. Never from Harvard to Yale. Ah. But that's for
kids."

He looked back to Carol. He said: "Time to grow
up, I guess. Me, too. You go home, I go home. What
was that book? *Childhood's End.* Remember the one you
gave me: *You Can't Go Home Again.* Christ. Nothing
makes sense today. Everything's gone haywire."

Carol was watching. She knew him well enough

to know that something large had happened. She caught it quickly.

"Billy? What happened?"

"I've been a nice kid, you know that? Big good-natured kid, all my life. We were great kids, you and I. Why is it, when you grow up, they can trade you? Parents can't trade you. But I guess that's been done, too. In the real game. I bet there have been people who traded kids. Christ, no, couldn't have been."

"Billy. Billy, what happened?"

"I got traded.

"What?"

"I just found out this morning. They traded me away, to another ball club out on the Coast. They say I'm over the hill."

"Oh my God. But I thought . . . you said they could never. . . ."

"That was back in the old days. When the Old Man was alive and I was young. He made the promise. 'I'll never trade you, Billy. Never. When the time comes to hang it up, you hang it up *here*, on my wall. This is your team. This is your home.' Ah. Everybody who knows me . . . knows that. I always said: If I'm not good enough here, I'm not good enough anywhere. When it's time to go home, just let me know. Well. They just did."

They sat in silence. After a while she said: "But . . . what are you going to do?"

He sat for a long moment. The answer was about to come, from the deep dark back of the brain. He said: "Strange thing about me. I never . . . I can't go to a new place, a new town, put on a new uniform, play hard and strong for somebody else. Not now. Not after all these years. The money . . . with strange guys . . . in a strange town . . . I just can't. So. What else? I'm going home. Just like you. Me and you. Going home."

They sat in silence. It took her a long moment to realize what had happened and what it meant to him, although she could not know how much she meant and could not ask, not now, perhaps not anymore ever again, and she stood up, beginning to shake, because they had moved into another world and she wanted to hold him but couldn't and was beginning to cry. She said: "Billy. Got to go. Good-bye. God bless."

She started off, began to run. He watched her go, made no move, sat there wooden in the cool wet air of September. Harvard came by once more, jogging toward a broken sunlight. Chapel: feels like you've taken one hell of a punch and you have to hold on to get through the round. He rose, walked out along the path, saw a field and some big trees to the right, felt raindrops falling slowly, lightly, and went over to stand under the trees, without lightning in the sky. No game today? Ah then, no choice. Home, Mr. Chapel.

But there's nobody there.

"You don't need me, Billy."

In the mountains, this winter, a lonely Christmas. . . .

There was only a light rain and he saw teams forming out on a baseball field a short way off, young

kids, a junior league, and a game was beginning without worry about rain, the sky was clearing.

Weather report last night had said it would be
clear in the afternoon.

There'll be a game today.

There were a few parents scattered along the side-
lines, a fat coach with a yellow baseball cap, an umpire
with a white shirt yelling something about getting the
game under way.

Billy walked over and sat a long way back under a
tree watching that first inning begin. All kids—not
even twelve years old. Dreamed of the early days, saw
visions of . . . the big kids coming up to hit . . . that
one kid who hit it over the fence that day, that crisp
golden day, with the bases loaded, over the fence, *foul,*
foul by less than a foot, and then, very carefully, threw
him the slow curve knowing he'd be going for it,
reaching, too soon, and he struck out, and Pops back
there, up screaming with joy: "Way to go, Billy Boy,
Way to go! All the way, Billy Boy, all the way!"

All the way.

Done?

A tug at his sleeve. He looked down: faces of three
very young boys:

"Hey, that's you! You Billy Chapel. Jeez! Hey, Mr.
Chapel, you gonna pitch today?"

THE
STADIUM

The stadium in that town was across the river, and it took a long while to get there in a cab. When Chapel arrived it was already jammed and he had heard the game was already sold out: it was. About eighty thousand people. All come to see the Yanks. To see the Yanks *win*. There would be almost nobody at all there from Atlanta, a reporter for the paper, some business types who just happened to be in town this day with nothing much else to do. But for the Yanks it was a very big day and the place was alive already with empty beer cans and signs being drawn and lifted and Chapel sat deep in the back of the cab while it pushed through. But . . . this really might be the last time. To come through the crowd up to the gate at the players' entrance with all the sounds, along with those silent drums that beat in the brain long before the game, steady, slow, heavy, marshaling the power. He had done this all his life: got ready for the game. Approached the game with that ritual of grandness, used to think of boys mounting chariots, just before the race, the trumpets blowing, the crowds gathering to scream and wave flags—wonder if they had known

that same impending wave of elation, the same joy of
collision ahead, just round the bend, back when they
played their own game a long time ago. This may be
your last time. But. You can watch television. Still
there was something dreamlike in the air around him;
he could sense the steadying of chariot horses, the
shining of the spears. All over. He brushed that aside.
Daydreamer.

Time to grow up, old daydreamer.

There are still two days of the season. Two days
in which to dream.

Nope.

One day.

Today.

Tomorrow . . . you'll not be here.

You can leave . . . right now.

Scheduled to pitch today.

You can pitch today.

Last time.

One more time.

He sat in the cab by the gate. Yankee fans all
round, alive. They have two games left in this season
and they're in contention. If they win today and tomorrow they go on into the playoffs for the World
Series. If they lose *one game* . . . that's why the manager, old Maxwell, is pitching you today. Because he
hates the Yankees. I wonder if he knows I've been
traded.

I don't have to pitch today.

I may well be . . . already done.

Ah. . . .

I could go back to the hotel and be gone, home in the mountains, up high in the Super Cub, by Sunday morning. Snow there already, light white. September snow, September sunlight. Fly the plane. Take the Cub and put down in the flat snowfields and go wandering, and maybe . . . think. Plan. People think you're slightly nuts. Flying up in *those places?* In the mountains? Are you out of your gourd? But oh . . . the clear blue sky when the wind was down, and the long low circling over the endless rock mountain, slowly down the long low lines between the ragged walls. . . .

He awoke. The cabdriver said: "Here you go, Mr. Chapel. They're waitin'."

A man by the gate who had recognized Chapel, was waving. Must have been told: get Chapel. Where's Chapel? He paid the cabdriver and walked toward the gate. The man there said happily: "Hey, Mr. Chapel, how you doin'? Good to see you. They gettin' a little worried so Maxwell sent me out here. They got you scheduled today, hey, man? Boy, this is gonna be a dilly."

Chapel went on by and down into the dark, through a cluster of people, nodding, pats on the shoulder, questions he did not answer. The door into the locker room was open for him and one of the locker boys scolded him, but it was very noisy and busy inside and so Chapel moved in through the locker room, his mind gone slightly blank, unable really to see who was there and hear anything that made sense.

Nothing yet clear. It may be for years, it may be forever. . . .

He felt a clutch on his shoulder.

"Chappie! Hey, man, how you doin'?"

He turned: Gus, anxious, nervous, worried, sad.

Gus: "Christ, buddy. I didn't think you was
comin'. Jeez, I thought, Billy's gone. He's really gone.
Oh, boy. That poor bastard, Ross, he's out in the hall.
He keeps bangin' the door. You want to tell him anything? You didn't see him when you came in?"

Chapel shook his head. Then another big face:
mustached, gray-haired: Maxwell, the manager: angry,
loud-mouthed.

"Chapel! Well, for Chrissakes it's about time.
Where the hell you been? Chrissakes, get out there and
warm up. Don't take your sweet time, we're goin'
right on schedule. Get a move on, man!"

He was gone, yelling toward a man whose name
Chapel did not place: "Listen, you, I wanna talk to
you, you gotta cut out that shit, you hear?" Chapel did
not hear what the shit was. He looked at Gus, and
suddenly—from nowhere—there was a smile, a spasm
of splendid joy. He grinned, patted Gus, went back
toward his own locker through the team, between the
black and white, the Cuban, the Puerto Rican, the
country boy, the city boy, the old pro and the young
dreamer, the settled and established and the scared and
the lonely. They said once traded you couldn't really
go back home to the old locker. If everybody else knew
it and you went into that room, it was not your room
and not your team and not your uniform anymore and

everybody knew it and you were some kind of alien, a man who didn't belong, and so most men once traded didn't come back, they just—disappeared, and the next time you saw them was on another field somewhere else in another uniform, and there was always some slight fragment of the old days, old memories, but . . . they were gone. From this game. The game that mattered. This one today. Always the one that mattered. The next one. The one not played. Not yet. The one we wait for. Today.

"Hey, Chappie, how's it goin'? Hey, man, you blow 'em away. You clean 'em up and lay 'em down. Man, I'd like to snuff 'em, Chap. I'm with ya."

That was Christopher. Nick Christopher. Team captain. Shortstop. One of the few good men on that team, an old pro who would be back next year and knew it and could therefore relax this day, in the locker with the losers, the last-place team. Most of them were here together but not together, would separate in a few days and see each other no more, some never to come back to the big league again, not ever. Near Christopher were the established few, the men who were good and had proved enough, or almost enough, to play this game in peace. But beyond them, and on all sides, were the others. Here on one side their smiling faces and jokes and kidding and over there was the sudden stillness, the strained faces, the anger, longing for the chance yet to convince *somebody* to give them one more chance, and then some with fate in their eyes, a certain peace, had resigned and let the chain go, would not be back next year and knew it, and since many around them knew it, there was that clear silence, that withdrawal from the . . . misbegotten.

Chapel walked through the room with nods and silence—it was normal for him not to talk much at all. They did not know of the trade. He thought about that. The trade was not yet done. Not yet real. Why? Season not yet over? The trade real only then? What the hell goes on in you, Billy? This is a business. Mucho money here. What the hell difference does it all really make? No one here knows it. No one looks at me as if I was a Martian. So. 'Tis only true if . . . if what?

He moved into that separate place in the locker room, always kept toward the back of the room for the Big Men, to prevent too much annoyance later by newspaper people. He went through the key men, beginning with Christopher, the shortstop, and they all gave that grateful hello and nodded, backed out of the way of that big man, Billy Chapel—on his way, that guy, to the Hall of Fame—one of the great ones—in all the record books. . . . Ah, Christ, if I could have been as good as Billy—he's made it, Billy, he's got *security.* Maybe with luck one of these days you'll make it, too, if you try hard enough. There was Manieri the third baseman and Dutch Johnson, the silly man with the mustache who told bad jokes and then laughed himself half to death while lying on the floor, a magnificent centerfielder, and then . . . Gus. Only friend. Only one who knows. No one knows. So. I am still . . . this is my team. One more time.

He reached his own locker—not his own, his visiting locker, his name taped high, and misspelled: Chappell. Gus was at his side.

"Christ, Chappie, I thought for a while. . . . Listen, that Ross fella, *what* do you want to do about him? You think you owe him? After all. . . ."

Chapel opened the locker door, saw his shirt. Gus went on rattling away.

"I thought: he's gone. He's on the plane right now and it's good-bye Charlie. I don't think anybody knows anything. Maxwell don't know. What do you think? He's got you scheduled today and he's a hard rock about it. He wants you, nobody but you. That kid Garcia, that skinny lefty from Puerto Rico, you know the one, he kept pleadin' for a shot, sayin' there's only two days left, and what the hell, we got nothin' to lose, which is a point, and he begged for a chance today against the Yanks, said even the big bosses would go along with him, to show his stuff, but Maxwell kept sayin', 'Not today. Maybe tomorrow. But not today. I go with Chapel today. And that's all she wrote. Got me? Now shut the hell up and sit down. I'll call you if I need you. Maybe in relief. That's what Maxwell said." Pause. "He sure hates the Yanks. You happen to know why?"

"No." Chapel lifted out his shirt, looked at the number.

Twenty-one.

Gus: "Chappie. What the hell you gonna do?"

"Twenty-one," Chapel said dreamily. He smiled. "They had a royal fight over that. Mom and Pop."

"Over what?"

"The number on the uniform. I've had that number . . . always. Since high school. My mother was an astrologer type. You know? And she wanted 9. She was sold on 9. But my father wanted 44. Don't remember why. But he loved 44. Then one day they compromised. Twenty-one." Chapel was dreamily smiling. "Twenty-one. They settled on that important number. At twenty-one you're a man. In those days. Vote at twenty-one. Drink at twenty-one. So, they got together. They voted. I've had that ever since."

Gus was staring at him.

"How you doin', kid?"

Chapel: "Oh. Who the hell knows?"

He turned, blinked, looked round the room, saw old faces which were no longer there, back in the days when he was young and had older friends, all the old pros watching and waiting with joy, and none of them there now, all of them gone, the days had ended . . . seventeen years. He was the last. Why was that important?

I'll not be back.

"You see Carol. Chappie?"

Chapel nodded.

"How'd it go?"

"It was . . . okay."

"You going to New Zealand? Or. . . ."

Chapel shook his head.

"Ah. Shit."

Chapel put down the shirt. Put his fingers along the front buttons. Stopped. Looked at Gus. Can't quit . . . today. Will quit tomorrow, but not today. He nodded. Nothing else was right. Cannot run now. Cannot leave *now*.

Gus: "Look. I think . . . if you don't mind . . . I got to tell that guy, that Ross, I got to tell him something."

Chapel nodded.

"All right."

"Yeah. But what?"

Chapel: "Gus. I can't quit today."

Gus stared, openmouthed.

"Gonna quit. Yep. No doubt of that. This is it. I go nowhere else. But I don't quit *today*. You understand?"

Gus, blinking: "Sure, Chappie, sure."

"So." Chapel held out his hand, raised the forefinger in the long, slim signal: One. He said, from deep in the throat: "One more time."

Gus nodded. He put out his hand, Chapel took it. Gus left.

Chapel put his hand to the right arm, held it round the muscle, talked to it for a long second: Old buddy, give 'em all we've got. The season's over. So. Are you ready?

He flexed the arm. Felt fine. He started to dress.

The team had already gone out when he finished; he was the last. He went slowly out into the sunlight and it was all fresh and clear, rain clouds were gone, a great day for the airplane, and he remembered that day he took Carol up and flew through the New Zealand Mountains, flew in a Cessna 182 with ice skis, put down on a glacier, the Franz Josef, and walked on hard, cold ice . . . won't go this year . . . so . . . wind today? Very light. Good. Give them no help with that. Everything on your side. But they'll want to win today. And my team. . . . My team? . . . won't give a damn. So . . . no matter. Does it matter?

Oh, yes.

Win the last one. Why does it matter so much? Don't know. But it does. But all you can do is your best.

I'll do that.

Only a game.

But today . . . today I'll throw it all, I'll throw all that's left because there's nothing to save anymore, no more rest to take anymore, today. . . .

He went to the warm-up circle where Dewey Bell was waiting for him. Bell was the reserve catcher, behind Gus. He could sometimes hit, he was a streak man, but he was not consistent and he did not have the arm yet . . . he had the brain. No doubt of that. Strange how so often . . . a great arm, an empty brain. He was standing with the glove, waiting to warm Billy up. A quiet man, waiting, biding his time, for Gus's job, because Gus did not hit. It was normal and natural and caused no pain. Most of them lived with that light in their eyes. Billy nodded hello, stared at Dewey Bell. Billy thought: I never had to live that way. I never went through that. Boy, the luck you've had. Well. Pop would say: "Play your heart out, Billy. Give it all back, Billy, everything you've been given. Give it all back . . . out of the golden arm." Pop's words. Give back the golden arm. And when it's all gone, you'll know, and look at it that way, Billy, there's no more to give . . . and you gave your best . . . always your best. From the golden arm God gave you.

Chapel shook his head. Cool it. Too bloody emotional. Cool it. Throw. Calmly. Think no more . . . of the heat of the sun, nor the furious winter's rages. . . . . No. Little music. Copland. He begun to hum, aloud, a tune from *Rodeo*. Took the clean baseball in his right hand, rolled the ball over, rubbed and cuddled and got the feel of it, touched it in that way he sometimes touched the wheel of the airplane, set the foot on the mound, took a good long slow look, set the distance, took a good long deep breath, then leaned back the first time slowly easily calmly, lay the ball back there behind him at the end of his arm, drawing the aim with his eyes, timing the body, focusing all things together, and he threw the first one.

It was faster than Bell expected. He jumped, but caught it, looked back quizzically.

"Hey, for Chrissake. Take it easy, you mind?" He threw the ball back. "You knock my hand off. Besides. You're too old to throw that fast. When you gonna learn that?" He looked over toward the Yankee bench, cocked his head to one side. "Oh. I get you. You scarin' the crap out of *them*. Okay. But gimme time to set myself."

First pitch too fast. Chapel: relax. Warm up. Better timing. He set himself and almost lobbed the next one, confusing Bell, but that didn't matter. Chapel was hearing the music in his head and conditioning himself, timing himself, sending messages all through the body, sensing the step, the push, the pull, the weight. All fine today. All good today. End of the season, hard slow cold season, they never scored behind you, but, no matter, you aren't weary today. That's a fact. Surprising. You have plenty tucked in there today. Must be a state of mind. I wonder . . . how far? Five innings? Six? Oh please God . . . today . . . if I could just go the distance. Let me go all the way. Give the old arm. . . . A rare thing for Chapel, who did not pray or go to church. But the desire was huge. He thought: be at least a little crafty, old man. Take it easy now. Rest and prime it. Save it for when you need it. Be crafty for once. Well. But best thing is blaze away at the beginning, put 'em *down*, boy, down, show 'em who's boss. *Then* get foxy. Sure. Waste nothing. Save the energy until you really need it, but . . . this is the last day. Today, you'll use it all. Sudden memory of Mom: "God has blessed you, Billy, with that wondrous talent. Remember someday . . . to give Him thanks." He never had. Well. May do it today. Right, Mom. But it's a little late. So . . . don't think on that. Music. And throw.

He went into the pattern of warming up, the pattern he had learned and followed for twenty years. The difference now was he could not quite relax. Something burning deep inside, fire in the chest. No pain. But chest a bit tight. Relax, Billy, relax.

Up came Maxwell. He was anxious and sweating, and kept both hands in his rear pockets, hunched over. He watched Chapel and the Yankees and the crowd in the seats, looked back over the dugout and saw the faces of the two owners and waved, and Chapel recognized that special nod and looked: the young men, sons of the Old Man. The ones who had traded him. Their seats were, naturally, just above the Hawks dugout. Chapel paused for one moment. Both waved at him. Smiles. He gave an automatic nod. Did not remember their names. Threw again. The Old Man . . . Billy started to call him "John." That was not his real name and at first it irritated him because the John was also the men's restroom, but Chapel automatically, definitely nicknamed him "John" from the first time they knew they were personal friends—which had become a habit of Chapel's; after reading *Hamlet* he began to call his mother "Gertrude" and the habit went on to Carol—so the Old Man responded with "Bobby," which was also not his name and which no one around them quite grasped. It was never explained, nor was that needed. In their own world, the Old Man and the boy, they were John, sometimes Old John, and Bobby, sometimes Roberto. In the office together, alone, out to dinner with a group, arguing, dreaming, planning, hoping, it was always John talking to Bobby, and there were times when other people tried those names—to be met with rage and silence. The two sons had tried— thought it their right. Chapel never answered. They still tried. The Old Man was gone. He had not been replaced. Until this day Chapel had not known how far gone he really was, thought of him always as out there in the bull pen, watching, or wandering up in the clouds, flying a small airplane, looking down.

There was a place up in high Colorado, an empty clearing in the northern mountains above Glenwood Springs which somehow was the place where John would drop in someday, when he came back. Chapel flew there in the fall, sometimes, landed in a small place in a Super Cub, sometimes with skis, and there was the place Chapel talked to the Old Man, and Pops, and sometimes Mom, and although he knew no one was there it was a visit Chapel had come to look forward to, because it was a lonely life, more and more, as you grew older on a failing team, loaded with slow ballplayers who would never join your "club" and were therefore never to be friends . . . except a few, who rose above that to be, somehow, a friend, without envy . . . or hope . . . those who still dreamed . . . like Gus. Only friend now, Gus. Carol . . . gone off to marry.

Throw harder. Loosen.

Oh where have you been, Billy Boy, Billy Boy?
Oh where have you been, charmin' Billy?
I have been to seek a wife
She's the joy of my life
She's a young thing and cannot leave her mother.

Again, Maxwell, tight and leaning forward, rocking.

"Hey listen, Chappie. I got a thought today. Today, I got this thought."

Chapel smiled very slightly:

"Good for you."

Maxwell: "Well, listen, old Gus always catches you, I know you fit together fine, but what do you think of this? What do you think if today we make a switch? Ha? What do you think?"

Chapel stopped throwing. Maxwell was rubbing his mouth, rocking.

Maxwell: "Got to hit 'em today. Just somebody up there swingin'. Hard. Gus don't . . . Christ, you know. This team don't hit, they don't back you up. But that other guy—what the hell's his name?—he can't hang in there like Gus and he don't have the arm, either, but Christ, off *you* nobody gets on base for a long time, so that don't hurt, not with you throwin', so I don't worry about that. Why don't we give Gus a rest today? Yeah." He nodded. "That's it. That's what we need. More power. We need more power."

"No," Chapel said.

Maxwell was looking toward Bell who was catching Chapel, and who did not hear this conversation, did not know he was the one Maxwell was talking about. He was crouching there peacefully, chewing, waiting. Maxwell did not notice what Chapel said.

Maxwell: "I wish to Christ we'd brought up that kid from the minors—hell, there are two different kids we're gonna try next year, from the South—" He swung to eye Chapel. "What?"

"No," Chapel said.

Maxwell stared, mouth open.

"Gus catches. Only Gus. You hear me. I hope. I hope to Christ you hear me."

Chapel put both hands straight down, one with

the glove, one with the ball, looked into Maxwell's eyes with a look that made Maxwell instinctively back away.

Maxwell said: "Billy. Jesus . . . what the hell's the matter?"

"I have my reasons. Gus catches today. That's it. That's all she wrote." Chapel signaled to Bell, started to throw again.

"Billy," Maxwell straightened, came vaguely, softly alert. "Billy, you tryin' to tell me how to run this ball club. *You*, Billy, of *all* people?"

"Nope. But Max, today . . . it's me and Gus. I need him. I never asked you any other time. Today . . . I go with Gus. Fine. Glad you agree. Don't want to fight now. Not today. No time. Today it's me and Gus. Right. Fine. Now let me warm up."

He leaned back, threw. Maxwell stood there. In silence. Chapel was ready. Will leave now, if necessary. Maxwell was watching him. Maxwell may have understood. Leave him alone. In a moment, Maxwell moved off. Then he stopped. He said slowly: "Okay, Billy. For you. Gus goes. But if we need a pinch hitter. . . ." Maxwell moved off.

Chapel began to throw again. Then there was another coming, a big Yank: Joe Birch.

He had been in the league almost as long as Chapel, had come up the year following, as a catcher, and he was one of the few truly great hitters. He was one of the big boys you met every now and then at banquets and he caught Chapel every year at the All Star game, and the friendship had begun a long time ago, when they began facing each other at the plate and leaving always with increasing admiration. They flew together sometimes, and hunted, and went out for a drink just to talk once in a while even though they'd never played on the same team. He was the best hitter Billy had ever faced. Billy had struck him out four consecutive times in one game. In the next game Birch had hit what may have been the longest home run in the history of his stadium off Billy's golden fastball. There was a joke going the rounds about something Birch once said after Billy struck him out with the third fastball, Old Smokey, the superfast number one into which Chapel put everything he had but threw only when absolutely necessary, and that one day he threw it right by Birch, about as fast as he'd ever thrown a ball, and Birch had turned to the umpire who'd called it the third strike—who was it? Meyers, Dave Meyers?—and Birch had said: "Dammit, Dave, that pitch sounded low to me."

Birch approached with a waving hand.

"Howdy Billy. How's it go?"

"Fine, Josephus. How's it with you?"

Chapel thought: but, it's not fine. Tell him? He'll know . . . soon enough. Him, too. Not long now. I hope. . . . Good luck.

Birch said wistfully: "Looky here, Billy, why don't you sit down today and take a rest. Will you do that? Tell 'em, hell, your arm hurts. Today. Do it as a favor. I swear to God, I'll strike out on purpose next game I see you. How about a deal?"

Chapel had to grin.

....

"Strike out? You? Joe, you don't know how. You'd swing without thinkin'."

"Well, I'd sure like to get into the Series this year. We gettin' on in years, you and me, and all these little boys around here, hell, why don't you just . . . take a break."

"Free shave today, Joe," Chapel said cheerily.

"Get ready to duck. Well. Luck, Billy. Good to see you."

He tapped the cap and moved off. Damn good man. Strange world. Never did figure. Talent doesn't go naturally with decency and warmth and kindness. Some of the good ones are bastards and some are . . . just fine. Doesn't go together. Some of the nicest . . . real bad ballplayers . . . doin' their best. What kind of world. . . . He glanced upward, toward the empty sky. You sure don't make much sense. But . . . I play it your way.

Dum dum. Don't talk to God today. Keep your mind intact, anyway. Nut. Enjoy the music.

He threw the last few. Time was approaching. He was done.

Warmth, peace, calmness in the arm. He put on the jacket and began the long, slow walk to the bench. The stands were rising, the genuine screams were beginning. Then came the performance: national anthem.

Introduction of the ballplayers. Big day. When they got to his name and he stepped forward there was a vast, surprising cheer. Billy touched the cap . . . to the enemy audience. Respect. A comedian somewhere:

I don't get no respect. He walked to the bench. They may never do that again. Calmly now. Better stop thinking about that part of it, if you can. Can you? I hope so. I hope to Christ I can settle down. Somehow.

One more time.

Song: Make believe you love me, one more time. For the good times. . . .

His own team was going to bat. The visiting team, hitting first. Chapel had the rough time, the waiting time. The man pitching against him that day was the Yankee ace, their best, Dave Durkee. People were still standing. Chapel was cheered that from inside the dugout you did not have to look at the faces of the owners. He pulled his hat down over his eyes, as was his natural custom and had been for twenty years . . . went into the quieting dark . . . saw the face of Carol. Lovely face. Blinked, opened his eyes. Felt a wave of sudden depression. No good to think of her now, not now. When this is over . . . there'll be time enough. . . . "Billy, you don't need me."

Love.

Do you love that girl, Billy?

What a hell of a time . . . hell of a question. . . .

Gus sat next to him. Chapel was grateful. Gus was gloomy, scared.

"Hell of a day, man, hell of a day. Christ, I wish. . . ." He didn't finish. He peered at Chapel: "How you doin', ole buddy?"

"Oh, fine."

"Stay loose, stay loose. Hey, how'd it really go with Carol?"

"Carol? Oh. She quit her job."

"Quit? She get into a fight with somebody?"

"No. She just thinks it's time to go home. She's . . . thirty-four."

"Hmm. But . . . she ain't mad at you?"

"No. But she said . . . she said I don't need her." Gus squinted. Nodded.

Chapel: "She was married once." Gus nodded. "It was a royal mess. When I met her . . . she swore never again. So we . . . we had a lot of fun, you know? We really did."

"She gettin' married."

"I think so."

"Yep," Gus nodded. "Well. Way the ball bounces."

The man at the plate popped up. There was a roar of joy from the crowd. Gus started latching his gear. Chapel said: "Funny thing, Gus. Funny thing."

"What?"

"We were never serious about . . . nothing. We were out to paint the town. And we did. Gee, she was . . . she was fun to be with. Always. But. . . ."

Third out. Gus stood up. But Chapel went on sitting.

Gus: "Time to go, Chappie. You ready?"

But Chapel said, mystified: "That was always the point. Have fun. Enjoy. But if you start to care for something . . . when you begin to care . . . that's what hurts you."

He stood up, shaking his head. "The thing you care for, that's where the real pain comes from. . . ."

Gus said: "Chappie? One thing I got to know. You gonna quit? Really quit?"

Chapel nodded. "Yep."

Gus: "No doubt at all?"

"No."

"Well," Gus said, "then whatya say we go on out and. . . ." He couldn't finish. He patted Chapel on the shoulder, started jogging off toward the plate.

Chapel pulled off the jacket, dropped it on the bench. He started out toward the mound. The Yankees were coming up. He heard the great roar from the crowd beginning, and then slowly, slowly, as he threw the last few pitches for the last warm-up, all that sound began to fade away, and he was alone . . .

THE
GAME

PART ONE

He put his foot on the rubber and the sound faded slowly away. He was no longer aware of the crowd. He saw no faces, no flags, heard no sound at all from the mass out there. He moved on into a narrow clear intense fascinating world. He could hear the thoughts of his own mind, always with a bit of background music, quiet music sometimes, flowing around through all the skull: sometimes he hummed softly, so softly that few people knew it because he was rarely heard. He moved into a time of intense concentration. He was aware of that hitter, him first and last, everything about him, his manner of standing, looking, moving, setting, and then of Gus behind him, the fingers of Gus's hand, the signals, then of the count, of the men on base, of the position of the team, of the umpires and their personalities and the looks on their faces and how they stood, of the *game*; of nothing else at all. He played every game in this way: from man to man, from pitch to pitch, aware of the way they stood, all their motions, with total concentration which excluded everything else, and the only other thing he had ever done like it was play chess a few times as a boy. As long as he had the concentration truly it was total: there was only the hitter, the game. When the concentration began to fade and the sounds came back and you began to look round and see all those other extraneous unnecessary things . . . then it was that you began to lose all the rest of it, the speed, the control, even the knowledge, and although you could last a bit longer if you wanted to hard enough and worked very very hard and had some luck, mostly you knew it was only a little while now till they started to hit you, and hit you, and it was time to fade out, call the relief . . . you were close to the end. He had pitched that way all his life; it was natural to him even as a boy. He moved into that other world as he warmed up. Then Gus came out to the mound.

"Umpire today is Dave Meyers." Gus pointed a thumb to the dark suit behind the plate. "That's good. Aint it?"

Chapel nodded. Meyers was a man who had great respect for Chapel. So much that if there was doubt in his mind about whether the pitch just thrown was a ball or a strike he usually figured that with Chapel throwing it was probably a strike, and he called them that way. It was a good day to have him there. Gus said: "Well. Boss. What's the word?"

"You know them all, well as I do. Same three. As always. Robinson first. Then Parrilli, you know."

"Right."

"But. One thing. I'm going to throw a little harder than usual."

"Gonna smoke 'em out?"

"Yep."

Gus understood. "Right. But take it easy. Don't throw it away too soon."

"Today," Chapel paused. "I'm throwing hard."

Gus looked at him for a long moment, then put out the ball, and when Chapel took it Gus held it for a long second.

"All the way," Gus said. Then he turned and ran heavily away: a big man, a round man, tucked himself in behind the plate.

Chapel looked down at the new white ball, rolled it in his hand. His mind said: "God is with thee." That was surprising; he had no idea where it had come from. He looked to the plate: the first hitter, Robinson, had moved into position, was setting his feet.

Billy Chapel and Gus Osinski worked as a team with their own signal system. Chapel had been in that league too long and knew too much to need much guidance so Gus rarely sent any signals. Chapel would stand motionless for a while, one long second, two, and Gus would usually anticipate the pitch and flick the finger signal for that one, and Chapel would nod his head or touch his forehead or his cap, sometimes even shake his head, out of that one long moment of immobility, so Gus would know what was coming. Gus rarely had to send more than two signals to get the right one and get back the nod, although Chapel threw a great many different kinds and speeds, but they had been together for four years, and for them it seemed natural. They both knew the hitters they were facing, would face, and talked much of them in the evenings, and unless someone new and unknown came into a game Gus knew what Chapel had planned and would throw. But there was one thing about Chapel as a pitcher which was rare and unpredictable.

Chapel had begun to learn as a boy that he could judge the hitter's mind by the motion of his body. Chapel would always study the hitter's stance, the setting of his feet, the motion of head and hands, fingers on the bat, and Chapel would know when the man was ready and when he was not, sometimes even know what he was looking for, outside or inside, or if he was set for the curve, and it was not noticeable that Chapel was doing this. It was a gift few pitchers had in their eyes as strongly as Chapel, and Gus didn't tell people about it but marveled at it himself. There were the eager boys who were often going for the first pitch, and they were the easiest. But then there were the big boys, those in a class with Josephus Birch, who almost never went for the first pitch, or even the second; they set themselves in there to watch and learn to time him that way, time the motion, and the first pitch was a gift and Chapel knew it and enjoyed it, but was careful to note the few times, the very few, when they were about to cross him up and go for the first one, to catch him off guard with a good clean easy one, and their message couldn't be hidden then, in the way they stood there, waiting, and he always knew. Whether or not it was natural to Chapel to pitch that way, and how much he'd learned by listening and watching, he never knew. But he did not waste pitches: he was economical. He seldom hit anybody with a pitch; his control was too good for that. He threw directly overhead and he was a tall man coming down off the mound so his blazing speed was speeding downhill, and yet sometimes floated, seemed to suddenly rise. He could throw almost anything—not the knuckleball—and there had been a scientific study of the big curve he sometimes threw which was described as moving along then "suddenly rolling off a table." Falling off the end, as Columbus supposedly expected to fall off the earth where the ocean ended. That was the best of the "sinkers." He almost never threw at the same speed twice in a row: he had been judged as impossible to time. Birch said once: "Against you, Billy, I always got to guess. Always. Mostly too late. Sometimes too soon. But ah, Billy, sometimes, thank God, I'm right." So with them all, but rarely at the beginning. Chapel began with speed and though he varied it he was always fast at the beginning, and they came up knowing that, and were without confidence in the way they stood, and it showed in their hitting: they were waiting for the later innings. And Chapel would throw the blazer often, early, but would vary the speed and every few innings would switch to sidearm, to a frightening fastball that was coming from a different direction. He had always been almost untouchable in the first few innings, and during that time most men knew it and did not truly set themselves, not until he began to slow, usually about the sixth inning. Then he would see them begin to move in closer to the plate and set the feet more firmly and he would perhaps switch to the sidearm, but not for long, because then he would begin to hear the sounds and his mind would wander and he would see beyond the hitter at the crowd, look through the screen at the faces of people, and then he would send the signal, and Maxwell would come out, and they would begin to stall enough to give relief time to warm up as much as necessary. That happened so often now, so often. But there was no good relief out in the pen anymore and so Maxwell was leaving him in too long, and so all this past year Chapel had been falling back like a soldier to a different position, closer to the sea, closer to the big waves, to where there was no place else to go. That was the feeling often in his mind. Now on retreat. Though he sometimes left them while still ahead he did not win them anymore, not with that same great consistency which had made him famous—even in fatigue he still had a magnificent fading charm—because the great basic weapon of that arm was always there and had not changed, not quite as strong or durable, drained too much by too many innings but with no real pain and no complaint, and he knew all that and had lost no faith at all. Chapel had great pride. As he stood up on the mound he reared back and cocked his foot high, very high, shooting up in a manner close to that of Marichal, a little like Palmer: men who faced him knew Chapel had confidence in himself, knew he would win. He brought with him an indescribable Presence, which was always there, always.

Robinson was ready: cautious, wary, watchful. Chapel began to hum silently: "Oh where have you been, Billy Boy, Billy Boy." Robby's never been a problem. Shortens up in the early innings—yes, he is now—hands move up the bat a trifle—hopes to squeak one through, get on base, short fly. Knows that 'gainst the fastball that will not do. Yes. Harder the better. Chapel smiled very slightly, cocked the arm, kicked the leg high, the fast one. Zip. Strike one. Robinson backed off. Chapel pocketed the smile. Now a bit faster. Pops used to call this one "Ole Smokey." This one was fast. All covered with snow. He blazed. Strike two. If that ever hits a man—Pops put his hat down over his heart, soulful, sad: "You hit him with that one, Billy, poor boy'll soon be in his grave, all covered with snow."

"Oh where have you been, Billy Boy, Billy Boy. . . ."

Gus was yelling: "Way to go, Chappie, way to go!"

Now. Robinson will expect it . . . outside. He's stepping in. Thinks I'll waste it. But doesn't know. Not for sure. Ah. No waste today. Throw it right by.

Chapel armed again and threw the third fast ball right by Robinson, who did not move, was not expecting it. Strike three in three pitches. Ah. A vague sound: Robinson eyeing him, lips moving as he walked away. In his motion: anger. Get you later, alligator. Always a next time. After'while, crocodile.

Next hitter: Babe Parrilli. Beefy Babe. Babe leans a bit forward, cocks the bat, but . . . he's seen Ole Smokey . . . a mite nervous today. Not truly set. Throw the curve right at him . . . so it'll break down and in. He did: Parrilli flinched back: strike one.

"I'm goin' away for to leave you, might not come

back any more more more, but if I ever more see your face again, there's honey on that far distant, di-istant shor-or-ore, honey, on that far distant shore." Kingston Trio. Long time ago.

Now: fire away. He threw hard. Strike two. Right down the alley. Parrilli backed off to tap at his shoes. He hadn't expected it. Next pitch, Parrilli thinks, will be the smoker again. This guy is throwin' nothin' but strikes. Set yourself. Parrilli, a gutsy man, dug in to hit. Chapel threw the sinker, it fell off the end of the table. Parrilli missed by six inches. Strike three.

Chapel backed off the mound, feeling a healthy glow. All working well. It's there today, buddy. Please God. For a while at least. One more time . . .

The third hitter was Jed Murphy. Along with Birch he was Yankee power. Chapel decided: total surprise. Sidearm fastball. Chapel never did that this early. Murphy backed away, startled. Strike one. Seven strikes in a row. Rather unusual. Yankee bench screaming: Chapel glanced that way: they were standing up. Ready to fight. Okay. He nodded, touched his cap. Chapel leaned all the way back, threw Old Smokey. Murphy never saw it. Strike two. The umpire, Meyers, was looking out toward Chapel, then shook his head. Quite an inning. Gus yelled: "Jesus, Billy! Jesus!" He crouched, then yelled again: "Nobody here but you and me, Billy, throw one more and let's go sit down."

Murphy knew the fastball was coming again, set himself, and Chapel threw the riser, the one that when held right in the fingers sometimes suddenly started to rise and float away and Murphy, set for one straight down the tube, went for it and just got a touch, popped it foul, and Gus wandered back, tucked it in, and the inning was done. In nine pitches. Should have been three strikeouts. Well. Nobody's perfect. They got only a foul. Pleasant way to start the day. Bit like the old days. . . .

"She'll be comin' round the mountain when she comes. . . ."

Chapel wandered back to the bench listening to nothing, thinking of nothing, resting the brain for a long moment. A good beginning. Power in the arm. He sat down in his normal place—the empty spot near the end of the bench. He sat alone, as always. Gus sat nearby, but Chapel did not talk. He sat, crouched far back, crossed his legs, tucked his cap down over his eyes . . . closed the eyes, floated off into the comforting dark, at rest, at rest, and he saw. . . .

. . . Carol. The blond hair. Down to the shoulders. Four years past, at the party, standing far across the room and still clearly visible, face lovely and weary and something dark in her eyes, seen from a long way away, but God in heaven, what a lovely thing. Movies? She wore something long and blue, bare down to the breasts, full round breasts, *tired*, she was talking to two expensive-looking men she apparently did not like. There was that girl Chapel was talking to at the time— dark-haired—who? No memory at all. Then—Carol appeared, facing him. Had come to see him. Curious. Weary eyes. He thought: drunk? She said, first words:

"You the Man of Distinction?"

"The which?"

"You look like that man in the ad. Man of Distinction. Did you pose for that ad? No you didn't. Nope. Who are you? Sir? If I may be so bold?"

"I'm a ballplayer."

She smiled. Mind beyond those eyes a total mystery. "A ballplayer? Dirty joke. Oh. 'Scuse me." Hand to her mouth, eyes with a glow. "That's right. You're the fella that throws real baseballs. The hero lass week. I saw that game." Eyes widened. Not really so drunk —or was she? "You were very good."

"Thank you, Ma'am." Western. Did that on purpose. Country boy. In New Yawk City. Charmin', thass me.

She said: "You struck out those three guys . . . one right after the other. With the bases loaded. That was . . . somethin'. I want to drink to you. Sir."

She was referring to that inning in the All Star game. He appreciated the fact that a girl as pretty as this one, however smashed she was, knew all this. She was saying, NewYorkerish:

"How much of that was luck? Truly?"

"Probably all of it."

Then she said suddenly: "Sorry. I don't mean . . . to be rude." Then she giggled, and switched right back. "On t'other hand. Ballplayers. Good pun there. I've heard a lot . . . tell me the truth. Are you gay?"

"Gay? Me?" He grinned. "Oh. You must have been readin' things. Or did you hear somethin'. . . ."

"Well, I know there's a lot of gay guys playing ball"—giggle—"nowadays. Is getting to be the vogue.

Or somethin'. So they say. Would you mind tellin' me? You know those fellas?"

"Nope. Honest."

"And you're not gay yourself?"

"Nope."

"But you fellas wander round nude all the time in the locker room. Does something like that . . . interest you?"

Billy started to grin. Then he had to laugh. He'd never been asked that sort of thing before, not by anyone anywhere, and she was from another world, and something in her face changed, and she looked at him with a sudden genuine smile, the haze in her eyes beginning to clear, something different there, and he said: "Hell. No. Nope. Uh-uh."

"Would you like to go for a walk?"

"A walk? Away from here?"

"I'd like to talk to you." She said that in an odd, intense way, vague glint in her eyes he did not understand. She said: "You're not married."

"No."

"I was married," she said. "Now it's over. I'm feeling the effects. Fallout. Would you mind if I talked? I can talk to you. God help me. If I'm wrong. Are you a . . . rebound?"

"A what?"

"Rebounds are people you go with when you've lost your love. True love. Shit. I didn't love . . . oh yes I did. But that was a long time ago. Would you walk?" She put a hand on his arm. First sign of great sadness. *Now* he saw. She said: "Please. Want to go out and . . . on the street . . . just talk. Need to clear a messy brain. Can we go? Do you mind? I don't mean to bed. I mean . . . can we find a place where I can just sit down and let it out?"

They left, went to a quiet bar. She told him of the ten years with that very wealthy lying conniving greedy vicious heartless lovable hatable son of a bitch who turned out in the long run to be very lucky that he never met Billy Chapel, who would have . . . "dusted him" . . . never marry again, she said, never never. You haven't ever married? Oh, Billy Chapel, you're either very lucky or very wise"—and Chapel said: "Neither. I'm a kid. A ballplayer. I'll grow up one of these days. But not yet, not yet. . . ."

Tap on the shoulder: Gus.

"Rise and shine, Billy. Number Two." Chapel came back into the game. Out toward the mound: no music: no pictures in the brain. All that cleared. He saw nothing but Joe Birch, slowly stepping into position to wait outside the box. Chapel's mind focused on Birch. Next man to hit. First up in the second: the clean-up man. Josephus.

Silence in Chapel's mind now rather unusual. Not the time for music. Vision: the swing Birch made that day when he hit it farther than anybody ever had before, that fastball, vision of the ball rising, going, departing, gone. Birch said afterward: "Never hit it that far except off Chapel's fastball. It was coming so fast I just closed my eyes and swung, and it bounced. S'truth, s'help me."

Birch stepped into the box. He nodded, from a

long way away. Chapel nodded. Meyers, the ump, said something to Gus, grinned, stroked his mustache. This would be interesting. Chapel stepped back off the mound: Gus knew: sent no signals, waited.

Chapel: sooner or later Josephus always hits you. He is one of the few, the very few, who gives you that slight clutch in the stomach that comes sometimes thinking of the way this one can hit the ball right back at you so hard and fast you may never see it coming, toward the head, as it did one time to. . . . Well. Fella has power. Great power. Almost never goes for the first pitch. Will he today? Look. No. Decisively no. Normal with Birch, but look: he sets himself and watches you and notes the wind and the thickness of the air—learned that from Williams—and all the details, and watches the first pitch with no motion at all, then two, slowly beginning to tick away to the timing zone that was just right, and then comes three, and by then he's ready, and he might go, certainly by four, don't ever ease up on four—but he often waits and walks, sensing properly the time when he'll get nothing at all to hit, so he might as well take the free trip, but today . . . no free trip today. Today: give him the best. And we'll see. Does he know? Think he does.

Well. Nothing better than the smoker. And today's the day. He won't expect it on first pitch. I almost never do. Because I don't want to give him the timing. So today: fireball one.

Chapel stepped to the mound. Looked again. Knew: he'll take the first one. So Chapel threw hard, right down the tube. Strike one.

Birch changed the position slightly. Ready now. He may go for . . . anything at all now. Yes. If it's close at all . . . the way he's set . . . hook to the inside. Off the wrist. The screwball. It took Gus a long time to find the right signal: even Gus wasn't expecting the screwball, which was not Chappie's best bending ball, at all at all, unless he was having one of those rare days when everything curved in every direction. Chapel cocked, threw, the pitch broke down and in toward the right-handed hitter: he swung, caught a tiny piece, fouled it back off his wrists. Strike two.

Haven't thrown a ball yet.

Hell of a day.

Yep.

What now, sonny?

Two strikes, no balls.

He won't expect one over the plate. He'll think I'll tease with a curve or a slider, like I just did. Why don't we . . . go to Number One?

Gus picked the signal. Chapel threw Old Smokey. He fired all there was, it blazed on by. Strike three.

Birch took it without any motion. Just stood there. He had expected something teasing, curving, bending, had been looking for the waste. He had struck out. He took a long look at Chapel, knew what was happening, put a hand up to his cap as a salute, went slowly away.

Three out of four strikeouts. Better settle down, ace. Can't go all the way. But gee . . . wasn't that fine?

No holds barred today, Billy. Throw it all, throw it all. Goin' home, Billy, goin' home.

Music came back into the mind now softly: Goin' Home, Goin' Home, I'm just goin' home. The symphony . . . of the New World. He began to relax a bit, now that Birch was gone, and did not go back to the fastball for several pitches, since that's what they all were expecting. It was unnecessary for the next two hitters. They were both tight, set for the heavy stuff, so he went to the big curve, the soft slider, and both grounded to the infield. Inning number two: done. Goin' Home, Goin' Home . . . walked slowly, happily to the bench, sat, tucked his cap down over his eyes. . . .

. . . they went to bed that first night—no—early in the morning. It was the wrong time. Too soon, too soon. There should have been more . . . time to open. She talked to him for hours about the mess of her life, she poured things out she had told no one else—she said: "I have no friends, and . . . there is something about you, something in that wide-eyed face." Across a crowded room. Something gentle and . . . innocent, the ballplayer, the big kid, and he was somebody she could talk to, and so she talked and eased out from under the weight of it that night and afterward she gave him her body, lay there as a social gift, did nothing but mechanize, exhausted, and he felt strange, missing links all over the place, because *that* woman, when you sat across a table from her and listened to her talk and watched her eyes move and glow and felt her hand come across to touch you, that woman was not the same one in bed that night. In the bed she was a robot. She watched him: she knew. She said: "Very sorry, Billy Boy." First time she called him that. "It was too soon." Chapel didn't understand why. But it was. She said: "I was doing you a favor, because you did one for me . . . but there's more to it than that . . . or should be . . . or probably never will be. You wanted more than that, and I don't have it, Billy, I don't have it. I'm a weeper. I don't have the right things . . . for anybody. Or was it—Billy—was it just . . . too quick? Was I too easy? Was that what it was? Because you are important to me already, you are not just another roll in the hay. What. . . ."

"I don't know what."

"Well, I'm sorry. I'll go. But . . . thanks, Billy."

"I'll see you tomorrow?"

Long look. "You want to see me tomorrow? Really?" She was genuinely surprised.

"Hell, yes."

She said: "We won't go to bed tomorrow."

"I want to see you. Do whatever. . . . Want to go flying?"

"I just want to have some fun," she said.

"I'll look into the matter."

"I think I can make you laugh. I betcha I can."

"How about flying? I know this fella who has a plane. Do you like to fly? I was thinking of flying up the river."

And they did. And it began. And they did not go to bed for. . . .

. . . tap on the shoulder. Gus.

"Less go, Chappie."

Chapel stood up, yawned dreamily.

Gus said, with a grin: "No. I mean it's your turn at the plate."

"Oh." Chapel looked round. Nobody on base. Hell with it.

Gus: "Now you take it easy. Durkee's throwin' in close today. Think he's tryin' to keep up with you. Shit. Never will. But we don't need nothin'."

"Eh." Chapel, who had always been blessed with a fine hitter's eyesight and excellent reflexes, was going to the plate not truly a good hitter but adequate, adequate: he knew where the ball was and sometimes guessed very well and had he gone into another position, not pitching, he might have had a pleasant surprise. Pops always believed that. With men on base Billy was consistent. But there was nobody on base at all and he did not want to use up the fuel by running, or even just standing there swinging, so he stepped casually up into position giving a happy cheerful peaceful grin, and Joe Birch, knowing him, said: "Howdy, Champ. Hell, you ain't takin' us serious."

"Josephus."

"What the hell you have for breakfast?"

"Scotch and water."

"Hmm. Know what? You get older, goddammit, you gettin' *faster*."

"Wait till next time. You ain't seen nothin' yet."

"Ah, come on. If that's true, I quit."

Durkee threw: right up the middle: strike one. Durkee understood. Ah. Why not? Chapel dug in. Durkee watched him, threw the next one far outside. Chapel chuckled. Durkee grimaced. Chapel said: "Tell him I think it's time I hit one. Yep. Time to swat."

They took him seriously and Durkee got careful and the next two pitches were fastballs, low. Chapel: don't want to walk. Hell, waste time standin' out there. Next pitch a slow curve: Chapel hit it on one hop to Durkee, didn't bother to run, just went a few casual steps and then turned and ambled back to the bench.

"See you, Josephus."

Birch laughed. "Hope I see you."

Chapel wandered back, but the inning was already over before he sat down; he stopped by the water cooler and drank that cool clear mountain dew, which was the kind the Old Man had started years ago and always tasted so fine on the warm days, and while he was standing there the next Hawk popped up, and so Chapel went back out for inning number three.

This was the easiest time, the bottom of the order: the last three men, the pitcher, and Chapel relaxed just a bit, began to glide through it all with some music in the brain and the pitching all clockwork natural, machinelike, precise, more and more instinctive with each passing moment, his head doing all the work back there in the dark overconscious part of the brain while Chapel dreamed along, firing away, not quite so fast now, that was unnecessary, not trying to strike them out anymore but getting them to hit one soon, pop it up, ground it out, foul it, and so it went; no one even got a fly into the outfield and the three were down. Chapel had a moment of splendid peace, warmth in the arm. A rare day. A fine day. All my life . . . this is what I was born to do. He sat . . . went back into the darkness. . . .

. . . and saw his father, Pops, catcher's mitt resting on the left knee. Twelve years old: Billy boy. Pop went out there with this big catcher's mitt and he'd move it around, and wherever he moved it Billy would throw until he hit the mitt. First the right, then the left. . . . "Always keep 'em down, Billy, except the wasters. And throw them *fast*. That's right. Keep *'em down*. If they have to go for 'em low like that they don't hit 'em straight, you see what I mean? The higher you pitch 'em . . ." he held the glove up to his chest, "the easier you make it for them. Oh, you fake 'em *sometimes*. A little too high. Too far inside. But *never* right here" . . . in the center of the chest. "Never down the tube, Billy. You move that ball around and shave all the edges, hit the corners, inside outside, never give 'em a good one, a soft easy one. But don't waste 'em too low, unless, well, now hit the *left* knee. Fastball, Billy. No need for the curve yet. When you're older. You wait for the curve, when the arm is ready. Come on, Billy. Ah! That was great! Right on the money. Ah, kid, you've got a future. So help me God, you've got a natural-born. . . ."

. . . they went out on this dirt road out in the

woods, and Pop had picked this one straight part as long as the rubber to the plate would be, and a place where the road had a natural mound where it came round a curve in the trees, and he and Pops went out there to practice . . . and Billy grew up. . . .

. . . driving one day in the mountains . . . Pop with Mom in the front seat and Billy, the only child, always the only kid there, no brother, no sister, none ever, never knew why, too late to ask, and he was always in the backseat and they were talking about him thinking he was asleep and wouldn't hear, but he heard, always to remember.

"Ah, lady love, but we're lucky. Who else is so lucky? He's such a good kid. Such a good sweet decent kid. And can he throw that ball. Godamighty, he's a natural."

"Oh he is. There's something just, well, just *nice* in our boy. Wonder who he got it from?"

"Certainly not me. Couldn't be me."

"Oh, you. You're . . . all right."

"Can't help wondering if sometime, if maybe God didn't have somethin' to do with it."

Billy listened. Pop didn't like church. Was against hell . . . and preachers.

Mom said: "Well, honey, you know, someday we maybe ought to let him just sit in at the church. People at school . . . some of the children laugh at him, you know."

"Nope. No church. Not yet. Not for Billy. They do nothin' but hellfire and brimstone, scarin' poor little kids to death, givin' 'em nightmares on how *evil* they are just thinkin'—*no*. Billy don't need none of that."

"But Billy . . . you know lately . . . the boy is alone."

Silence.

Pop: "He does love . . . the game."

Mom: "Yes, but. . . ."

Pop: "Tell me this. Now tell me. Do you think he plays . . . just for me?"

Mom: "What? Land sakes. . . ."

Pop: "No. I mean it. I love the game myself. And Billy knows that. And he's such a sweet kid. Do you think he goes out there . . . 'cause I want him to?"

Mom: "Now. Ridiculous."

Pop: "Honest."

Mom: "Well, maybe he started that way. Maybe it helps him. Yes. I think it does help him. The way you root for him. But you know and I know and now everybody knows, that boy is *good* at pitchin.' And he knows that, too. It's . . . natural. And he's lucky to have that. To be so good . . . as good as he is."

"Ah, that he is. Oh, lady, isn't he *somethin'*? You sit there watchin' him and everybody gets still, because he's in a class by himself and everybody knows it, he's on his way. . . . Because you know what I feel? That little kid back there is gonna make us so proud . . . so proud. . . . And he wins . . . you see him come home so happy. I hope to God. . . ."

Mom turned to check her sleeping son: Billy closed his eyes. She thought him asleep, tucked a blanket round him, put a warm touch to his forehead. He was never to forget that moment in the backseat, those words up front from Mom and Pop, from whom there had come a gentle childhood. Mom worried, Pop cursed . . . and they loved him. Chapel sitting on the bench in the dark felt a surge of emotion, opened his eyes. Goin' Home, Goin' Home. . . . But they're not there anymore.

Nobody's home anymore.

Carol's goin' home.

Carol's gettin' married.

He saw a Hawk batter strike out. Shucks. This here team . . . doesn't hit much. At all.

Game is: nothing—nothing.

Gus was tapping him: time to go.

Gonna win this one. Gonna give 'em hell today. If only the folks . . . but maybe they know. Gee, if only they could be there, somewhere.

Out at the mound he tried to clear the memory of Mom and Pop. Focus on the hitter. Go to music: yes: Copland, then, word by word, a song from Neil Diamond. It went on automatically as he stood there in deep concentration, the music flowing by as a stream beside him, keeping him company all the way down to the end of the game, would be always there unless there was a tough situation . . . if men began to get on base, but there was nothing tough at all this day. Down they went like dominoes—but one man hit a fly ball to center, longest ball of the game, but high, not far, and slowly adrift: Johnson wandered over lazily and tucked it in. So Chapel went back and bore down, and all the while, in harmony with the pitching:

You had reasons a-plenty for a-goin'
This I know, this I know,
For the weeds had been steadily growin'—
Please don't go, please don't go. (Strike three!)
Are you goin' away with no word of farewell
Will there be not a trace left behind?
Well I could have loved you better
Didn't mean to be unkind,
And you know, that was the last thing on my
mind . . .

Billy eased back, went to the sinker, got the last man on a high hopper to second. Back off the mound. . . .

. . . a good song. Lesson too late for the learning. I am, I said. Fella used to love Neil Diamond, too, was Old John, Big John, the Poor Man's John, the ancient owner of the Hawks who'd owned the team when Billy was born: there he sat with his feet up on the desk, as usual and natural, smoking that cloudy pipe, blowin' the damned smoke in all directions all over the room, wearing a spotted tie, loose, as always, wandering around the field always in a white and spotted shirt. Springtime. Old John said: "Roberto. I must tell you . . . the Plan."

He had the custom, whenever he used those sacred words, "The Plan," of pausing first and turning his head first left, then right, making sure he was not to be overheard. He'd gotten it from an old movie. He said: "The highest tab any player gets in this game this year, so far as I know, is. . . ." He gave a number. He did the same thing every year. Then he'd say: "I can at least match it. How's that?"

Chapel would say, "Fine," and they would drink on it, and so was the contract formed every year, from the first year on, for fifteen years. Chapel did not get an agent. Baseball was changing, but he did not change with it. He had his talk with the Old Man every year and the lawyers drew it up as instructed. Sometimes the Old Man would say wistfully, "Roberto, old kid, why don't you sometimes just argue a little? I mean, even a *little*. Hell, you could push for more, just a little, probably. You know that."

And Chapel would smile and never answer. And they knew why, and the Old Man liked that part of him very much. Billy was young and clean, fresh out of the old days. He had all the money he needed, and land and a hotel out in Colorado, and even money out of commercials, and the rest of it was all headaches and taxes, and mathematical complexity, and he had begun with the Old Man, played his first game in the major leagues because the Old Man came to see him and shook his hand, and the team he played for belonged to the Old Man, and the Old Man, Big John, was Head Coach. To Billy Chapel, all was in order and he did not argue. He was a very good pitcher. He was becoming a great one. But toward the end there were many gathering complications, and the Old Man, who saw it all coming, began to warn him.

"Billy, Roberto . . . one of these days I ain't goan

be here no mo . . . to settle with. You got me? You and me, we have this here now 'verbal' agreement that's good as Gibraltar right now, by Jesus and Christ, but . . . *but* . . . the times they are a-changing. Billy, go get yourself a legal representative from t'other side and get all the fine points written down. Listen. You do that, sonny."

"Okay. But I don't need it yet."

"Roberto, someday. . . ." But he did not say: "I'm dying." Could not say that. Though he knew, he knew. . . .

A hit. Chapel knew from the roar next to him on the bench. Opened an eye: somebody had singled, a bouncer through the hole at short. On first base. Who? Ernie . . . Italian fella. Right fielder. Well. Go ahead, folks. Blast away. Chapel closed his eyes.

"Earth receive an honored guest." Carol quoted that when the Old Man died. In the spring . . . when the season, two years back. . . . Rise and Fall. She talked of civilizations. History buff. Good to listen to. But made him think of the Old Man and the team, and the game itself: teams rise and fall: the great days of the old Giants, the Yankees, the Dodgers, the Reds, they all come they all go. Odd. But in the beginning . . . those early days . . . so young, and the big guns forming around him; the Hawks were on the rise, and glad to see him come, and many friends then, many close friends behind you and with you afterward in the bar or in the restaurant or out with the girls that came in flocks: days to look forward to a possible World Series, to hope and plan and wonder, and then you did it: victory. And then again. The Old Man with the champagne. Hugged Billy: "Kid, God bless you. At times like this . . . oh, God, there's nothin' to say." Joy in the locker. Golden Age. Did it again. Billy won three games in the World Series. Came on as a reliever in the eighth inning of the last one and blew 'em away. The Old Man boomed: "Talk about contract this year, Billy. We give you half the team."

Then the big boys slowly began to depart and Billy was past thirty and more and more alone, because the younger players did not feel comfortable with him—the Old Man explained that one night: "Billy, you been up ten years. You are as close to the heart of this team as any man can be, and they all know it. Always remember, Billy, that the better you get the more lonely you'll be."

True.

Why. Never understood. Carol: jealousy. Talk like a woman? She said: "Billy, you're too lucky in this life. You have so much . . . they'll never have. You know that. You love it."

So. There will be an answer: let it be.

The last few years, the team went steadily down. Decline and Fall. The Old Man was tired. Did not really try anymore. Let it be. But it did get a bit lonely. Except for Carol. Made a hell of a difference . . . another roar. Good God, another hit. Ernie going to third. Make it? Christ. He did. Well. Interesting.

But Chapel had learned not to waste energy rooting. Backed away. Think of something else. Harder now. Saw the Old Man. At his home in the mountains.

Went fishing there all those years, together in the boat . . . . Old Man on a fly rod. . . . "Billy, when the time comes I think you'll know it. I don't think nobody will have to tell you. When you haven't got it anymore you may know it all of a sudden in one day and you may have to see them hit the ball over and over, but Billy, I leave it up to you. You go when you're ready. You tell me. Okay? Agreed? But nobody will ever push you. Never. You done too much for me, kid, in all these years. Except . . . why do you call me John? My name ain't John."

"Your name is Burton."

"Yeah. Isn't that awful?"

"You don't look like Burton. You look like John."

"John who?"

"Just . . . John."

"So. Sometimes I call you Roberto. But you know what? You ain't really Roberto. You don't look like Roberto."

"Who's Roberto?"

"Oh. I got it out of old Hemingway book, war book. Good book. I forget the title."

Earth receive an honored guest. . . .

Just before he died . . . wanted to talk about it. Couldn't. Wandering. Didn't stay on the same subject. But one day he said: "Goddammit, Billy, when I'm gone go out west and get a gunslinger and come back here with *force*, or they'll get you, kid, they'll *hurt* you, all that legal . . . minefield . . . a goddam minefield."

Chapel: I never planned. Couldn't think of him

gone. He went the same year as my folks. Rise and Fall. Must ask Carol someday . . . why does so much have to end in pain? Why can't a man just reach the high point, and then . . . explode in Technicolor . . . in his chosen place, on his chosen day?

Carol: close now, that lovely face: "Billy, why do you love this game? Only a game. But you love it so."

. . . tap on the shoulder. Gus. What did we get? Nothing.

Ah, but I do love it so.

He stood up. Gus was talking, Maxwell had come over to say something, warn him about something to which Chapel did not listen. Did not need. He was getting waves of emotion now. This was going to be a strong day. Love all this. Walking out to fire away. Today . . . something sparkled in the air now. Something different now. All systems are Go—as Pop used to say. There were no mistakes, not even errors behind him, the control was damn near perfect, and he was threading needles with blinding speed, deceptive curving stuff, functioning with that magical sensation of total control, as if he was flying way up on a clear day and the plane was smooth, the air like glass, all the ticking steady steady, loving the white clouds, the little white specks on the windshield. The difference . . . All this will pass. Last day. Don't think on that. Live every moment, Billy. Ah. Here comes Birch. Know what? You'll get him. The music stopped, all systems slowed, the drum moved to a different beat, and

Chapel was wary, foxed Josephus, got him to go for the sinker and trickle it back to the mound. *Two.* Relax a bit now, drift off and let the machine purr and wind and fire—Copland now, *Rodeo*—and he began to back off the mound to look up at the sky and rest for one moment, one short but total moment, just looking at a round white cloud.

Then for the first time he looked down at the team —from man to man in the infield and then out to the broad outfield, something he rarely did, or needed to do, all that was for Gus and the manager, but now . . . his eyes came back into focus and he looked with care.

Something different.

They stand . . . alive.

They seem to have come alive. Why? They're *eager.*

Amazing.

All this year, all the last few weeks . . . they just sort of stood there, waiting for it all to end. But now, today . . . beat the Yanks? Is that it? Well, whatever.

But they sure are different.

Good feeling.

But at this moment Chapel felt the first weight of real fatigue. Too soon. Too soon. There is much left, but . . . one must shift the gears. He stood resting for a long moment in the great silence, breathed long breaths of cool calm air, shifted his gear in his own quiet way, grinned at the team—he felt a fine difference now—then turned back to pitch.

···

Music came on when he returned to the mound, a soft clear voice in the back of his brain:

"Don't look so sad, I know it's Over"

He fired with rare intensity. Strike one.

"But life goes on, and this old world will keep
on turnin' "

He stopped for a moment, rubbed the ball in his hand.

"Just be glad for all the time we had together,
there's no need to watch the bridges that we're
burnin' "

He pitched then to the rest of that tune, the music and the words flowing on with every pitch, and he was throwing with smoke:

"Place your head upon my pillow
Hold your warm and tender body close to mine
Hear the whisper of the raindrops fallin' soft
upon the window—
And make believe you love me, one
more time—"

No more of that. He cleared the head, stepped back, then whirled and threw sidearm for a rare time in the game and struck out that hitter, and Gus let him know on the way to the bench that he hadn't even seen that one comin', and: "Jeez, Billy, signal me sometimes, will ya do that? I'm havin' a charmin' time trying to hang on to some of these things, but I tell you. . . ."

Chapel looked up over the dugout and there again were the faces of the two sons who had traded him. He glanced quickly away. "Over the hill." That's what they'll say. Fresh blood. Young blood. "Make believe you love me, one more time . . . for the good times." He sat, the hat came over his eyes, but the music went on . . . one more time.

Tap on the shoulder: Gus.

"Go hit him, Billy. Make the bastard work for a livin'."

"My turn . . . so soon? Well. Won't be long."

Up to hit again. What inning? Makes no difference.

Chapel walked straight to the plate, wasted no time in the circle. But he began to focus on Durkee. Aha. Chapel's mind cheered. Durkee, I betcha, this time will make the first one a strike, somewhere over the plate. Oh, hell, almost certainly the fastball, yes, the fastball. Try to finish me in a hurry, thinking I'm resting. Well, by Jesus, not today. Today, ole chap, we go the whole damn way.

Chapel set himself, dug in. Wonder if Durkee notices? Or Joe. But they didn't. Durkee came down the tube with the first pitch: a fastball, which Chapel hit—crack!—a line drive straight to center. Chapel took off running but hit too hard—and right at the centerfielder—who moved only a step or two, and took the ball in. Hit on a straight and solid line. Ah, son, bad luck, no luck hitting thataway. If it was only a little softer, it would have fallen in, or if you were swinging a little faster, you'd have hit it longer, and over to left . . . let it go. Forget. Maybe next time. But next time . . . he'll be careful.

Well, good. Make him work a little bit.

. . . saw Carol on skis in New Zealand, learning the "flight" downhill, and that time she took off like a wobbling bird and the skis began to rotate, and she went tumbling along through flying mounds of white winding snow, and he was after her and fell on top of her, face-to-face half covered with snow, both of them, and he had rarely laughed so much, or felt so sexy, in other places, other times. Couldn't make love at that moment: too many clothes, too much snow. Observers. Breathless. Blue eyes, stunning face, teasing him: oh but darling, how can you let this moment pass? I want you I need you have mercy. And with her hands probing, seeking, giggling away. Afterward . . . in the hotel she sat on the bed in a blue nightgown, ah, so beautiful, outlined against the wide window and the mountains and the snow. She said—she was holding a glass of—champagne?—she said: "You ever been in love with a girl, Billy?"

"Oh, sure."

"I mean in love. Really."

"Yep. Honest."

"Who was it?"

"Girl in high school. Sheeee. . . ."

"Well. What happened?"

"Nothin'. To be exact."

"Crud. Why not?"

"Oh . . . she was beautiful. A little dark doll. And the figure . . . ah, me."

"Well. Did you go out with her much?"

"Nope. Not at all."

"Not at all? Why not?"

"She was Jewish."

"Jewish."

"Yep."

"My God. You're not serious."

"Yep."

"And for *that* reason you didn't go out with her?"

"Oh, no. Not her. Me. She wouldn't go out with *me.*"

Broke up in laughter, collapsed on the bed. She asked, filled glass balanced in her hand: "Are you part Indian? Tell me truth. She wouldn't go with a . . . Comanche?"

"I never went to church. To tell the truth. My folks didn't believe in Hell. My pop used to say. . . ."

"Tell me the truth. You from Denver, from the Rockies? You my half-breed?"

Chapel started to laugh. In her face then there was a marvelous curiosity he was never to forget.

She began to insist: "Now don't be hurt. I don't mind. I mean . . . oh, hell, is *that* what happened? Was she one of those people against Indians?"

"Won't tell you."

"Oh come on."

"Nope. It very old, very hard secret. I promise. No tell. Ever. Ugh."

He was moving into her, remembered that, remembered. She was saying:

"You really an Indian? No kidding? Which tribe? How much Indian?"

"No tell." He crossed his heart, then hers. They began to wrestle and it became a rare time, and he was inside her and he said, whispering: "Okay, the truth. You make good squaw. Honest Injun. Let's . . . ride."

She wrapped him in her legs. "Geronimo!" she yelled, and he broke up laughing while making love. "Ride hard. Geronimo!"

"Me not Geronimo. No. Not him."

"Who was it? In your family? Really. Who?"

"Me . . . Crazy Horse."

They laughed for a long time. She said: "I can feel the resemblance."

"I thought you were gonna say Sitting Bull. If you'd said Sitting Bull . . ."

Afterward: "You Crazy Horse. Me Jane."

Off she goes . . . to marry, marry. . . .

Up to go out again. Sing no sad songs for me. Memories were blending now into the pitching, and it was a magic blend: he would fire away and remember her touch, and fire away and remember the joy of holding, loving, without thought, with vast desire, and at the same time the mind clicking quietly calmly practically majestically along, cutting them down, one, then another, not one hit, one that gave that solid sound that made you turn with apprehension to see where it was going. Me Crazy Horse. Chapel's Last Stand. Finished the inning. Music—Oh where have you been, Billy Boy, Billy Boy—walking toward the bench, felt the arm of Gus around his shoulders. A sweaty delighted excited anxious face:

"Hey, man, how you doin'? How you feel? You okay? Jesus, I tell you, Billy, I've never seen you better. You goin' through them all like . . . God amighty. You . . . man, how you doin'?"

"Okay."

"Now you pacin' yourself? Good. Glad to see that. For a while there you throwin' every damn thing so hard I was getting nervous myself."

"Not so's I could notice it."

"Billy . . . I never seen you better. You worry me. You're throwin' your heart out. All right, all right. But man, if you can keep it up . . ."

He sat.

There is a trace of weariness, old chap.

How long do you think?

Pace yourself.

Yes.

Watched Christopher go up to hit.

Gee. If this team could get a run . . . that's all I need.

Feel no more the heat of the sun, nor the furious winter's rages . . .

Where the hell was that?

"Thou thy earthly task have done, home art gone

and ta'en thy wages . . . golden lads and girls all must, like chimney sweepers, come to dust. . ."

Carol . . . reading that . . . fireplace some- where . . . wintertime . . . golden lads and girls all must . . . like chimney sweepers, come to dust . . . .

. . . one time she dated somebody and went to bed with him.

How did you know?

I knew.

She dated a lot of people. No. Not a lot. Seemed like a lot.

You didn't own her.

We never owned each other.

Always free . . . and yet . . .

One time . . . she went to bed with . . . who- ever. And the way she acted, you knew. So you asked her. She said yes. Very cold. Do you mind? No word at all. You did mind. She knew. She said: won't happen again. You said nothing. She never asked you who you were seeing. But from almost the beginning . . . you didn't see anybody at all. . . .

Love.

Have never used that word. To anybody any- where . . . except the folks.

The girl that I marry will have to be . . .

The biggest fool in all history . . .

One day in her office, she said: "Dammit, Billy, you're certainly no dum-dum. Why don't you read a few things? You've had no education but high school and God knows that was no education where *you* went to school, but you have a fine mind, really, Geronimo, sweetie, I want you to read a few things. Hokay? The basic stuff. Just a few that *everybody* should read.

She had much of it already, because she had that job at the publishing house and did a lot of reading herself and had books all over her place, and she began pushing things to him, she seemed to need it, and he was grateful. Because perhaps he'd reached the right age to read things he'd never gone into as a kid. Some were very good, many he'd never heard of, and some he'd heard of and was supposed to be in awe of he did not like at all, so he assumed he had poor taste and it would have to develop and that would take time. But he began to read more and more when he was away from Carol, taking the books with him to the hotels during the season, getting him a reputation with the team as a bookworm, and then one day: *Anna Karenina.*

Carol: "You don't like it? *Tolstoy*, you don't like? What the hell is wrong?"

Chapel said: "Well, the way I see it, *she's* okay. I mean, Anna. She's good. But the guy she falls in love with is a cluck. I have no sympathy. She gives her life away for a cluck."

"A cluck." Carol was staring at him. No idea what she was thinking. Then she began to laugh. She laughed very hard and then came and put her arms around him. Then she whispered in his ear: "That's what all us clever women do. We give our lives to clucks." Chapel was oddly hurt by that, and she knew, she knew. She took him to bed where they always eased all pain. She was good at that. She was . . . the best. She made him feel that day as if . . . but the word she did not use. He never used it, either. One day she was drunk. She said, he remembered her dull eyes: "Love. Getting to be dirty word. Don't believe in it anymore."

"I don't know. Sometimes. . . ."

"How many people you know—hic—really love each other? I mean . . . *really?* Really and truly would die without the other . . . like—hic—Romeo and Juliet?"

"Well now, *that* one is by Old Will, and with that fella. . . ."

"I think people need each other for a while, and that's what they call it. Love. When a guy needs to have a girl to screw and boost the ego, and he finds this doll, for a while there things are mooney-spooney, and she's that way with him, and it's all some kind of weirdo joke. The girl goes with some guy for two weeks, three weeks, and raves about him and dreams about him and then suddenly sort of—wakes up, you know what I mean, and she asks herself, My God, what did I ever see in that guy? It's all some kind of genetic code."

"A what?"

"Genetic code. Find the right guy, like any female animal, to father the necessary kid."

"No kidding."

"Yep. Thass what they all do. Right guy. Kid comes along and they need that because the little thing needs them, and it's love like between Momma Kitty and the little kitties. All for a while, but then the kitties grow up, and nobody needs you. Love is . . . need."

"Hmm. Have to think on that. I sure did love my folks."

"Oh sure. Genetic. You needed 'em, but *you*, Billy . . . you love the game. Don't you? Truly? I mean, you're the most happy fella . . . out on the mound. 'In't that true?"

"Yep. I think."

"What do you love? Can you tell me that?"

. . . at that moment there was a base hit: he opened his eyes, somebody on his team had doubled and was pulling up at second. Well. Getting to Durkee? No, I don't think so. Durkee went back to the heavy stuff. Chapel closed his eyes.

. . . Carol said something about . . . all life . . . a crazy game. And Billy said: "No. It's more than a game. If you play right."

"Meaning? In a hundred words or less. What is there about baseball, that . . . special type of game, as it were, that you so love and adore?"

"Very funny."

"No. Really." An odd strange wistful look in those wide blue eyes. Aha. A mystery. Of what that thing is that a man could adore.

"Well." Pause. "Gee, this ain't easy." Pause. "Best I can explain . . . when I go out on the field, I go out . . . *all of me*. I mean . . . the best moments I've ever known were the times in an important game when they had men on base in the late innings, scoring position, and their best hitters coming up, and you stand there and take a deep breath and then you give it all you have, all you have, and you don't fool em, oh, no, not just that, nothin' foxy about it, when the big times come and the big guys step in to hit, to win, and you throw it *right by them, pop*, the sound of that thing belting the catcher's glove, the sound of . . . *strike three!* Ah . . . those are the moments you look forward to . . . and they're always waiting just a little way ahead, every guy steps in there to hit, and you put 'em down, but not all . . . you don't expect to get 'em all, but it's there in every moment, every pitch, the possibility they'll hit, and they sometimes do. But mostly no . . . yet sometimes . . . I guess that's the main joy of it. I'm good at it. Yes I am. And maybe . . . mmm . . . never thought of this . . . the other thing I love is the airplane . . . up in the high and lonely blue. I go up there to wander and dream and relax . . . rest . . . wandering through clear air between the clouds when the air is soft and smooth, no bumps, and you can see all the way to the end of the world. Then at night you play the music and dream of the good times . . . which are coming again."

He blinked, opened his eyes, jolted by his own mind.

"Make believe you love me . . . one more time . . . for the good times."

Music of that next line: "I'll get along . . . you'll find another . . ."

Wonder who she'll marry. Will I ever meet him? Will she be happy? Someone she needs?

"Billy, you don't need me."

She said once: "Billy, tell me, other than my butt, is there any one thing about me you like? What's the best thing?"

"Oh, that's simple. You're fun to be with. Every time you show up, I begin to smile. And . . . I don't mean jokes."

"I see. Me. The sunshine kid."

"Well. Is there one thing about me? Any one thing?"

"Your strength."

"What?"

"I don't mean muscle. I mean . . . first thing I could see . . . in your eyes . . . what you call 'a tough cookie.' I thought: this one's a tough one. He doesn't run from trouble."

"Ah, well. That ain't exactly strength of mind."

Gus: tap on the shoulder. Something about the next hitter. Chapel nodded, not listening. He thought: Philosophy . . . one day he told Carol . . . remember? . . . that the book that impressed him the most was that German . . . Immanuel?

She said: "Who?"

"Immanuel. Last name is. . . . Don't. No. *Can't.*"

"Immanuel Kant." She pronounced it "Kahn't." He said: okay, Kahnt. She eyed him with considerable thought.

"Well. What do you think of Kant?"

"Right on the button. He says that when people see the same thing happen, they see it with different eyes, and remember different things—although they all saw the same thing."

"Critique of Pure Reason."

"Yeah. That one. He's right on the nob. My father said the same thing. Used to warn me. People see different things."

"Your father?"

"Yep. He was a cop, you remember."

"Oh. Oh, yes. Cop. Deputy?"

"Both. He was a very good cop. Everybody knew that. Proud of him. And I'll always remember the way he'd talk about interpreting witnesses, the way you could pick people up who were *there*, who stood there and watched while the crime happened, and yet they told you different stories you had to sort of, *filter*, and yet they all would believe exactly what they said, and sometimes their memories would change in a few days, too, and they'd remember it differently but that wasn't necessarily *lying* . . . no point in getting mad at people for changing memories. It was just that people saw with different minds . . . and saw sometimes what they wanted to remember seeing. Just about the same thing Kant said. Good point."

"Golly," Carol said.

Chapel's memory smiled.

"Oh ye," he said, "of little faith."

"No, Billy, no I'm not. That's one thing I have faith in. . . ."

Later she said: "You are my . . . big little boy."

"My boy." She said that. That she said.

Child. Heart lies still but blood's a rover.

Straighten up, child.

But she said . . . *mine.*

Change the pitch. Think of . . . flying.

She liked it. Really did. I remember at the beginning she barfed, after the flight. I thought: she's only doing it for me. But she went on, and, gee, the girl has guts. . . .

. . . his mind began to chuckle.

The Mile High Club.

Ah, yes. Did that . . . where?

In Scotland.

That one day . . . going up out of Inverness and heading west, toward the Isle of Skye . . . in a Cessna 150, a little bitty airplane which they would let me fly as a rental only by making me a member of the Royal Club, to make it legal, which it really wasn't, and oh, it was a bumpy day . . . we were bouncing along over the Highlands, round spots of snow in the rounded mountains, when he mentioned the Royal Club, and how it reminded him of the *other* club, the Mile High Club, grinning away over pure and lovely Scotland, and Carol said: "How do you join that club? I mean, can *I* join that club?"

"Oh very difficult. Very very. You gotta have a lot of heart and guts and desire . . . oh, yes, *desire*, you gotta have that"

"For what. Tell me."

He explained that the Mile High Club was a very exclusive club joinable only by people who had managed to make love in a small private plane at an altitude of at least one mile: 5,280 feet. In a private plane it was very difficult, especially to have room enough; and also, it wasn't cricket to do it with an auto-pilot, that was considered "bad form."

She was mystified, examined the Cessna. They were not far then from Loch Ness. "How in hell . . ."

"Well. Maybe not this kind of plane. Need something a trifle bigger. But it's distinctly possible that if we. . . ."

"Are you a member of the . . . Mile High Club?"

"Matter of fact (embarrassed) no."

"Never found a co-pilot who'd have you, eh?" She was meditating. Then she began taking off her blouse. She said: "It'll be cold in here. Turn up the heater."

He turned up the heater; she removed the blouse, then the bra. He admired. He said: "Hope we don't have to make a sudden landing. Scotland is a bit . . . conservative."

"Well." She regarded him with interest. "Guess there's only one way. I have to do all the work. Billy, sure you can control this here airplane while I . . . go to work? Joining the club?"

"How do you figure . . . ?"

She put her head down in his lap. She said: "Do you think this will qualify us?"

"Gee. I don't know."

"Well. Far as I'm concerned. . . ."

She went into action, with that lovely, masterful mouth.

And so they joined the Mile High Club.

They rented planes everywhere they went, overseas. Flew in New Zealand, up on the glaciers. Flew up the Rhine, round the Lorelei. He asked her once if she could picture herself as an old maid and she said: "Oh, sure. I'm going to live in this beautiful little house in the country, surrounded by a high wire fence, loaded up with books and cats. Cats and books. Once I get out of the big city . . . You, Billy? God. I bet you'll be the old man glued to the TV set watching ball games all day all night. Do you root much? I mean, the games are noisy enough, but do you yell and scream and throw things, like my father does, and spill beer all over?"

"Hell, no. Oh, I won't watch. Not me."

"You won't? You're kidding."

"Nope. I just don't like to watch a game I can't play any longer. I can't just . . . sit there. That happened to me after I left high school and didn't play basketball again. I wasn't tall enough, so if I went to a game I found I went nuts just sitting there, so I didn't go anymore, and TV wasn't . . . well . . . maybe a little. But I just couldn't sit there and *root*, you know? Yell my head off. Not natural. But *football* now, maybe yes. I never did play much, so I can watch and enjoy. But *this* game, baseball, once it's over, it's really over."

Chapel opened his eyes. Suddenly, abruptly, rather tired. Stared at the team up the bench. They seemed . . . unusually intense, wanting to win. Odd. Something strange in all the faces. Looked to the plate and at that moment the hitter up there went into one, caught it good and hard and deep, and Chapel himself hopped to his feet to see it go. . . . Very unusual for him, but the ball had been hit and he saw it rise and rise, and go and go, and he thought for one long lovely matchless moment it was gone, up over the fence and far far away, but it started to come down just a bit too soon, one hair too soon, struck the top of the fence and bounced back in the field and they played it quickly and damn near got the man going into second base: *Gus*, of all people, old Gus had hit that one and made it to second base, in flight all the way like an airborne battleship. When he slid into second he knocked the baseman down, and—temporarily—out, and they needed attention out on the field and there were ugly remarks but big Gus stood out there with that huge grin, sweating away from the run, although it was late September weather and a cool day. Chapel watched with great hope. A nothing-nothing ball game, every play tight at a normal time, but today—Gus was very slow, and even if there was a hit—Maxwell was on the edge of the bench thinking of taking Gus in for a pinch runner, but then, all too quick, a pop foul: the catcher, Birch, circled under it and tucked it in and it was over, no score again, another man left. But Chapel was happy for Gus. Doing his best, that guy. May someday learn to be quite a hitter, if he works at it. Tell him that? No.

Gus came out to the mound, puffing. Chapel took time now. Let us all rest a bit. He said: "Man, that was close. I thought for a minute there. . . .

"Me, too. Ah. Wouldn't it be loverly? All I want is a room upstairs."

Gus was nervous, rubbing his face. Chapel took note of it but it meant . . . approaching the end. Well.

Throw hard, Billy. He warmed up slowly, giving Gus time to get his breath. Phrases from Carol . . . all came back:

> Fear no more the heat of the sun
> Nor the furious winter's rages.
> Thou thy earthly task have done,
> Home art gone and ta'en thy wages.
> Golden lads and girls all must
> Like chimney sweepers, come to dust . . .

Carol read that. Several times. Never forgot it. Didn't know who. Shakespeare? Golden lads and girls all must, like chimney sweepers, come to dust . . . our revels now are ended. . . .

No more of that. But the music now in the mind was quieting. Harder to concentrate. He thought: there is still time, brother.

Who said that? Quote from where? Can't remember. . . .

. . . remembered:

"Mr. Chapel, I'm sorry."

Highway Patrol, at the door. Big tall fella who had known him and Pop since . . . long time ago. Hat off, held it in his hand. Tears. Remember: all things come to sharp clear focus. You take a deep breath and the heart rolls over.

"Your folks, Mr. Chapel."

Pause.

"Yes, sir. I'm sorry."

Pause.

"Happened about an hour ago. No hope left. I'm
. . . they just went off the road. They've been taken
in. If you want me to . . . do anything? Drive you
in?"

In that moment, no motion. You take the time in,
Billy, and let it come in and go by and out the other
side, and then you must move. And you say, I can
drive myself, because you really must be alone and
that you know. You put on the hat and the coat,
against the cold. Oh, it will be cold. And you say:
"They went together?"

And he understands.

"Yes, sir. They went together."

"Well. I think . . . they'd want it that way."

. . . later somebody wanted him to identify and
Chapel refused, and some official was surprised, irritated, because everybody did that when necessary, it
was a duty, but Chapel did not do it, and walked away.
To look down upon a mangled face . . . I have been
hard in my day, but I am not hard enough for that, I
might just crack across the brain. I have looked well
enough before, and will remember what I have seen
. . . always. Will not look now at what I do not wish
to remember, with these eyes—Dad used to say, "My
God, Billy, but you've got great eyes! That's where the
control starts, in those great blue eyes!" And Mom
hugged him and said: "Pretty blue-eyed boy. So
pretty." And so that day Chapel went off by himself
and started to cry, and was left alone. And he remembered Pop saying: "If ever that day comes, Billy, and

I'm gone, always remember, I'll be waiting for you somewhere, somewhere up ahead, and it won't be long, won't really be long. . . ."

Tap on the shoulder. Chapel turned, woke. What inning? Bottom of the seventh. Nothing—nothing. You sure. His eyes were hazy. Not good. He thought: "over the hill." Not quite yet. If I can go just a little bit farther. . . .

PART TWO

When Chapel threw the first pitch in the bottom of the seventh he began to feel pain in his right arm. That was unusual for Chapel: fatigue yes, weariness of course, but pain he rarely felt, and never for long. Weariness of the muscle was easy to recognize and even to foresee, to feel *coming*, but pain was a sudden signal, rare and always abrupt, the clear warning: cease, desist. The big red light.

Chapel backed off the mound. When that had happened on other days he would signal Gus and Gus would come out and then maybe Maxwell also . . . but today . . . tell no one. Today . . . it doesn't mean the same. Today must go on.

Hmm. Reminded him of a book, of *The Old Man and the Sea*, the way the old man sat out there with that one bad hand that the old man felt sorry for, because it had worked so hard all his life and was pretty much useless now . . . odd thing to think about. Worn and weary hand, out there hooked into the big fish . . . he felt an astounding sympathy for the old man. Know what you mean. Because there was a pain in his right arm, beginning in the elbow going up into the muscle above that, leading to the shoulder, and there had been times when he'd gone on, talking to the arm, pushing it, coaxing it, scolding it, as he did in the World Series, saying: buddy, not now, don't quit now, and sometimes it kept going long enough, and sometimes the pain got much worse and he had to quit, so he talked to it now, said: "Just this time. Just this last time. Sorry old buddy, but today we must go all the way, and we haven't got much more to go, so if you have to hurt a bit that's all right, but let's give them . . . the best. Get the last few. Only a few.

But it was more than a few. He went to the fastball. Easiest to throw in some ways; the curve could cause more pain. Remember Koufax? The fastball was what he couldn't take. . . . Don't think of that. They've been waiting for you to slow down for six innings, and look at them now, they're waking up. So fire Old Smokey, and if it's there . . . please God. . . .

First hitter in the seventh was Robinson, dug in now, waiting with eagerness now. Chapel struck him out for the third straight time. The fastball was there and no mistake. The pain was there, too, and it was new to be this way, to throw hard with pain in the arm. In the past they worried and sat him down as soon as possible and the pain never lasted, was always quickly gone, and he remembered the Old Man's fear. . . .

But Old Man, there's nowhere else to go today and there's nothing more to lose . . . he apologized to the fine and aging arm as that reliable veteran who had the power still struck another one . . . Parrilli again, gee whiz, wonder how many. Lost count. Doesn't matter. Bless 'em all, bless 'em all, the long and the short and the tall . . . turned round and glanced at the infield and . . . something strange happening. Different position. They were all tensed and crouched and bobbing up and down and yelling. He could begin to hear Christopher screaming, as Christopher almost never screamed: "Go get 'em, Billy Boy, Blow 'em away, Billy. You got 'em, Billy, you got 'em," on and on, never ceasing.

A rare thing.

They didn't get excited, near the end of a game, not this team. They were a tired team in the seventh, all except Christopher, and Manieri, and sometimes the Dutchman. They did not expect to win and so it had not really been a contest in a long time and almost never had the motion and energy he saw now. No more playing with a stacked deck. Got a chance to win.

Chapel felt shortness of breath. At your age, old buddy, when it starts to go . . . He threw the curve and backed off Murphy, who was expecting the fast ball. Sidearmed him with another ball. Then threw the third straight wide breaking curve which fell outside and Murphy reached far enough to touch it, and hit a meager ground ball to first and was out by half the length.

Done.

Seven.

Chapel came down off the mound and walked toward the dugout . . . and the concentration began to go.

The pain was in the right elbow going up through the shoulder. As he put his left hand over to probe, to soothe, his eyes began to wander anew, and suddenly, abruptly he came into focus on all those people watching. He slowed the walk and looked up across the stands and they began to come to life, moved back into sight; the sound broke through the barrier and he could hear the great boiling hum of . . . eighty thousand people. The yelling, the rooting, no special words, all now bedlam, going into the top of the eighth, could not even hear the voice on the loudspeaker. But he had lost it now . . . he had come out of that quiet world of total commitment and control was gone now, no longer in complete control and knew it. Seven innings . . . as far as we can go. Time now to warm up the relief.

But not today.

Two more innings.

What you think?

Got to.

No doubt at all.

Got to.

Wonder . . . how far you'll get.

All the way.

So help me God.

Sonny boy, thou canst not make two more.

Well. Give it a try. Will do that. Am going out now. Yes. He nodded. There may be enough left . . . we shall see.

He looked over at the Yankee bench. Tension and motion; they were steaming. Pressure from that bench. They really wanted . . . feeling from that way came as a wind. Was a quiet surprise. He sat wishing it was . . . more quiet. Too damn much noise. He looked up and around, down the bench, no longer pulled the cap down over his eyes, kept running his hand up to his right shoulder. The pain there was growing as he sat.

He was still very much alone at this end of the bench. He looked down the bench now and the nearest was Garcia, the young pitcher who had pleaded with Maxwell to give him a break earlier, before the game started. Garcia was not looking at him. He was sulking, gloomed, one foot against a post. He had no interest in who won that day. Not unless he pitched. Well. He may. Chapel said: "Hey."

Garcia swung, startled:

"Ha?"

Chapel remembered, a long time ago, when a great pitcher, Sam Johnson, began sitting there on the bench lecturing to him about the big things he should know. But Chapel was foggy now in the brain; this was instinctive. He wanted to talk, to somebody. He said: "Hey, young feller. When you begin to hear the crowd, that's time to quit. You ever notice that? Long as you don't notice the crowd, you're all right."

Garcia was staring at him, mouth open. He shrugged, said something in Spanish. Then abruptly he got up and moved away, sat down on the bench, talked to another ballplayer, pointed at Chapel and then Chapel noticed much of the rest of the bench staring at him and talking. He knew: I have pitched one hell of a game. They're wondering . . . I never let up. They didn't think I had it in me. I. . . . Over the hill? He chuckled, but both arms across his chest. Not yet I ain't.

Two more innings.

Rest. Drink the water. Eat some candy, ice cream.

He went to Gus and got the Babe Ruth that Gus always had sitting there, near cold water. He always chomped on candy in the late innings. He didn't say a word. When Chapel came near everybody quieted. He went away again, sat alone.

All right: rest. Every bone, every muscle, the eyes. The brain. Send the resting signals down: right leg, left leg, and on around. Pain only there, in the right arm. Better now. How much reserve?

No way to know. From the back of the brain . . . a slow dark signal from deep down there, way back where the dreams formed and much of the work was done. There's not enough left, Billy Boy, Billy Boy. They're going to get you.

Well then. He took a cool breath. Why don't this team get a run? Just one. Even one. The salubrious effect, the message to the brain would spark all the way down. Learned long ago: you do the best you can. If they don't score behind you it doesn't help to get mad or sad or lifeless . . . and yet . . . strange thing . . . if they *do* . . . if they only back you up. . . . But Durkee had gone to his reserve, was throwing all the best. The Hawks went down.

Bottom of the eighth.

Chapel waiting, just sitting as long as possible, before beginning the long walk out to the mound which was now dangerous. Things had changed. He had lost much of the power. They had been waiting all day for the golden time: it had come. Chapel went out . . . and began to hear from his own team: alive and ready for the brawl. Out there to win. They were all looking his way and yelling encouragement. Maxwell . . . did not come out. Maxwell did not say a word. Odd. Stood above the bench watching, waiting. There was real tension here now, almost as if the World Series was under way and this game was the heart of it—as if it was one of the few games, the very few, out of all the long years of all the long games, the few that really and truly permanently mattered, and Chapel felt a choke in his chest. He had a team behind him. "Go Chappie go Chappie . . . !"

Somebody from the stands. Them, too? For *him?* What the hell. . . .

Gus was waiting at the mound. Ashen face. Twitching. Chapel, hazing a bit in the brain, looked at the scoreboard. Instinctive message, before he looked, come from that dark place there in the dreamy brain, the place that followed the game and knew it all.

No-hitter.

He focused on the board. Nothing-nothing. But the numbers behind that, under: Runs, Hits, Errors read clear and bright: Hawks: 0 Runs, 4 Hits, 0 Errors. Then underneath, for the Yanks: 0 Runs, 0 Hits, 0 Errors.

In the early innings . . . but this was the eighth. Chapel said, aloud: "Gee whiz."

Christopher, the shortstop, came running up to the mound. He had the ball in his hand, the one they'd been tossing around the infield. He had a wide-eyed, formal, very tight face, and he handed Chapel the ball, held his hand for a long moment, saying, through gritted teeth: "We gonna git 'em. We gonna git 'em. Anybody drops the ball, so help me Christ, I'll kill 'em. Go 'head, man, I'm right behind ya."

He ran back to position, hopping, skipping. Manieri at third was crouching, pounding his glove with heavy punches, yelling something untranslatable. Italian? The man at second base stalked like a readying leopard.

Gus said: "Chappie? Listen. Joe Birch. Time for Joe Birch. What you wanna do?"

Eighth inning. Birch up for . . . third, or was it fourth time? Only third? He looked past Gus, saw Birch, standing, leaning slightly against his own bat, like a cane, motionless, looking out toward Chapel. Waiting. Chapel thought: know what? This is serious. It was as if he was waking up. All this was . . . clear and real. A well-developed picture . . . of a ball game. Chapel put a hand to the right arm, the shoulder.

Gus: "How you doin', Ace?"

"Little tired."

Gus nodded. "You got a right. Anybody got a right." Pause. "Well, Chappie. It's Birch. Whatya wanna do?"

Chapel blinked. What now? Nothing came.

Gus: "Listen, this guy's always trouble. You never . . . lucky. How 'bout walkin' him? Everything outside. Far away. So's he can't—"

"No," Chapel said.

The umpire, Meyers, had begun to move slowly out toward the mound. No more delay. But he came slowly.

Gus said: "You've slowed a bit, Chappie. Just enough for this guy to get you. Hell, let's put him on."

"Not today," Chapel said. "Any other day . . . maybe . . . but today . . . Gus . . . ah . . . I can't."

Gus gulped, put out a hand, patted the ball in Chapel's hand.

Chapel: "Gus, it's the last time."

Gus: "Right. Well. I'm with you, Boss. Throw . . . throw hard."

He turned, started back toward the plate, met Meyers, who looked at Chapel and gave a friendly nod, and went back with him.

Alone on the mound.

No-hitter. That complicates things a bit.

Oh, hell, I've been here before. Dozens of times. They always get to you . . . in the late innings. Count on nothing. Gee, it would be nice. He shook his head. Think no more . . . of the heat of the sun. Think of ole Joe. Hiya Joe, watcha want? Joe had stepped into the box, was setting, as always, with that patient wait for the coming explosion. Well. May never do this again. No time for caution. Go out with pride, Billy. Only way. He set himself, summoned up strength, leaned on into it, and threw the fastest pitch he was capable of throwing. Strike one.

Pain burned the shoulder. Joe looked back in surprise, shook his head, backed out, came back again. Chapel could hear the crowd beginning to scream. Distracting. He stopped, took a long breath, then did it all again, gave it everything again, and it blazed. Joe swung and missed. Too late.

Chapel: one more. If I get Joe this time . . . I'll go home happy.

Joe knew it was coming. He stood for a moment in doubt, searching Chapel's stance, setting himself for a fraction of a second without certainty, and so Chapel did it again, the last time, and it went right on by and he swung late, not believing in what he saw, and he was out of there and Chapel felt a spasm of great joy, great pain, and backed off the mound to breathe and rest and thank God.

The infield was pitching the ball around and Gus came out.

"Wow." Shook his head. "I tell you. Listen. How's the arm?"

"What difference does it make?"

Gus looked, nodded.

"Okay, Boss. They can't . . . they can't touch you."

Chapel got the next two. The arm was beginning to burn, but it was working perfectly. Don't much matter now. Medicine tonight, no pain tonight, take a long rest . . . yes, a long long rest, he promised the arm that, and so gave it all he had, and one popped up, but the last one caught the ball and hit a liner to deep center, the hardest hit ball of the day, but it was not far enough, and too high, and Johnson drifted easily gracefully under it and tucked it in, put it away, and the eighth was done.

A long way to the bench now. The crowd had quieted, was watching him: he felt the eyes. One more to go. Last inning. Last day.

Don't think of that. Just three more. Think of them. But . . . all will be pinch hitters. Maybe not. Think of . . . Carol. Is she watching this? On the TV tube? I hope she is. I hope I get those three. Oh, God, if I get those three . . .

Now at the bench no one would talk to him at all. They moved away into a bunch and rattled to themselves. No hitter. It was the code. Don't mention the words. Magic words. But all aware. Shut up. Play with the heart, not the arm. Because the arm, old buddy, is a-weary. Goin' away for to leave you . . . not *you*.

He touched then held the aching arm.

Three more. Just those three. Can you do it?

You can do it.

Well at least old friend I'll give it a hell of a try.

He sat. Blank the mind. Push the button, as you do in a computer. Blank it all. Rest. But he had been concentrating all that day on each hitter as he came, one man at a time in total concentration, and now that had changed, it was no longer one hitter to be faced; the game had come alive, the world round him had begun to breathe, was *real* now in an awakened way, and so finally he realized the thing that was happening. It came out of that black darkness in the rear of the brain, intruded into the clear light of day. He thought: *can't be.*

He sat up, straight up. Turned, saw Gus. Gus was chewing on a fingernail: an unusual thing for him to do. There came a sudden tremendous roar from the crowd: the bench erupted. Chapel turned: Christopher had hit one: going, going, Christopher had rounded first, on to second, the ball hit the wall, high up, careened, Christopher rounded second and headed for third. Chapel began to scream, first time in years: "Make it, man, make it, gotta make it, *slide!*" Christopher hit the dirt, made it easily, safely, was in with a triple. The whole bench was ecstatic, was moving out in front of the dugout, roar from the crowd was gigantic, even the home crowd, very rare, very rare. Christopher had tripled. Chapel searched the board. One out. He could score on a fly. Please God. The old pro, Christopher. Under pressure, he does it. Maybe I can. . . . We're going to get one. He started clapping his hands. Maxwell was hopping back and forth, yelling to people. Pinch-hitter?

Out there was: the Dutchman. Chapel heard Gus screaming: "Get it out of here! Get it *out of here!* Lift it, lift it, lift it!" Chapel came up next to him, tapped his arm; Gus turned, blanched.

"Go 'way and sit down, dammit. Rest, rest."

"Gus?"

But Gus went yelling to the Dutchmen to hit it— and the Dutchmen did. Long fly ball. Durkee had tired enough, just enough. A fly to the far right. There'll be time. Christopher had tagged. The fly was caught—too far away for hope for them . . . Christopher came home and scored.

The elation of the team was the same as . . . a long time ago. The past was briefly back. Ahead now. Score: 1–0. "Gonna beat the Yanks!"

"We got 'em, we got 'em. You, Chappie, sit down! we gonna get 'em!"

He sat. Ah. Have not felt this way . . . if I can hold three more . . .

Gus was putting on the gear.

Chapel: who's coming up? Bottom of the line. Last three. So. Will be pinch hitters. All three. Who the hell? Brain a haze, no memory came. Clear the head, old pro. The arm slowed on that last one or he'd never have hit it to center field. How much . . . time do you have?

Then came back the slow cold clear message:

Nobody on base.

At all, at all.

Third out came. The team was moving out, yelling to him, at themselves. Chapel stood.

Thought: may well be the last time I ever do . . . stand here.

No one on base? For eight innings.

He started the long walk. He said slowly, to himself, to the arm: one more time: Kid, you do your best, you can get any three guys that ever lived.

There was Gus at the mound. Chapel said, smiling: "Howdy."

There was Christopher, white-faced. Chapel said: "Thanks, ole buddy. Appreciate it."

Christopher, as intense now as Chapel had ever seen him, said through those gritted teeth: "Listen, you . . . you . . . but if I drop the ball myself, so help me, I'll kill myself. You . . . give it to 'em, Chappie."

He was gone.

It was quieting. Quieter and quieter, all over the field and the stands. They were beginning just to sit silently and watch. Very few cheers. Silent sound in the quiet air. Gus stood there just looking at him.

Chapel said: "Gus? How many have they got on base."

Gus sort of shuddered. He said: "Nobody."

"Oh. I wasn't sure."

"Didn't think you were. But everybody else . . ."

A perfect game.

Chapel: "This I haven't seen much of."

Gus: "Me neither."

After a moment Gus said: "Chappie, I never have."

"How many there been? How many guys ever pitched . . . ?"

Gus: "I don't know."

Chapel: "Six or eight. Maybe a few more. I remember . . . Catfish Hunter. Few years ago. Larsen, at the World Series."

Gus nodded. Meyers was waiting back there, but this time he did not come out to get the game moving, he was going to give Chapel all the time he needed.

Finally, Gus said: "Chappie, we're all with you. All the way. You see the guys . . . you know. Three more to get. Only three. Throw anything. We'll get 'em."

"I've slowed down a little."

Gus nodded. "Just a hair. Be careful."

Chapel: "I think I may have thrown . . . all I've got."

Gus put a hand out on his shoulder, squeezed.

"Buddy, you throw. We'll take care. Whatever . . . go on, buddy, go all the way like you've done so far today and you can't lose . . . never."

He moved off.

Chapel was alone. With eighty thousand eyes on him. Well aware of that. Uncomfortable. Shrug it off. He did.

He backed off the mound, took off his cap, rubbed the sweating brow. No one on base at all. No walk, no hit, not even an error or anybody hit by a pitch. Nobody on at all. Nobody. So unusual a thing. . . . He looked up at the sky. Hadn't prayed since childhood. Time for it now. He said to God: "Sir? In all my life . . . I never wanted something as much as I want these three. If you can help . . . I won't be here again . . . you know how much I love . . . if you can help a little . . . just these three. I never asked before. But just these three. Please. I'd be obliged."

He put the cap back on. His lips hadn't moved, he was flushing and could feel it. Hope they didn't see that. Well, does it matter? Nope. Nothing at all mat-

ters. Except the three guys comin'. Gonna get them.
So help me God.

Saw the face of the first pinch hitter: Bum Neil-
sen. Does not hit well, but can hit the long ball. Why
him now? Stupid. What they need now is a man on
base. Ah . . . they think I've slowed, and he can hit
the fastball. Very strong on the fastball. Well, no
fastball. Dinky do sidearm, screwball best of all:

Two fouls. A pop up to third.

One down.

Jubilation behind him.

The right arm was going numb. Gus came out.
Chapel saw Maxwell making signals to the outfield,
moving them over. He did that when he knew Chapel
had slowed and the hitters could begin getting in front
of the ball and pulling it.

Gus said: "Who the hell's this next guy? You know
him?"

Chapel squinted.

Fella called Sparky something. Fast. Chapel said:
"Watch the bunt. He may bunt."

"Right. What you gonna do?"

"Sidearm. Easier on the arm. And keep the ball
rising."

First pitch worked. He tried to bunt, popped it
foul.

Second pitch got away: wild pitch, sailed over
Gus's head to the screen. Gus came out to calm him.

"Jeez, Chappie, don't hit nobody. Don't give 'em
the goddam base. You okay?" He looked toward Maxwell. No relief, goddammit. Not now of all times.

Maxwell made no move. Thanks, Max. Gus said: "Sidearm curve, again, again. Okay? Okay."

He went back, crouched. The curve did not break well, almost caught Sparky in the head. That was close. But . . . go back now to the fastball. He knows you're losin' control, he'll be tense and won't dig in. Chapel went back to all the fastball that was left. It worked. Strike two. Hard to bunt now, he'll be swinging now.

Chapel threw the fastball past him, struck him out.

The crowd all over the stadium was standing now. Chapel's right arm was beginning to send stabs of intense pain. A little while, just a little while . . . but if this next guy gets on . . . don't let him.

How?

Nothing came now, no plan.

Hitter was McClendon. Good man.

Last hitter.

I hope to God.

I got him last time . . . with the sinker. He won't hit first pitch . . . how can you tell now . . . and hates the sinker. So. First pitch: fastball.

The pitch hit the ground in front of the plate. Gus came out, talked. Chapel went back to the fastball. Untouched. Strike one.

The sinker.

Untouched.

Strike two.

Noise beginning around him.

One more time.

Curve broke outside. A ball.

That's a rare thing.

Can't even walk him.

Chapel realized he had had given everything he had, was close to collapse. Vision fading. Oh, hell, just one more pitch.

There was nothing much there. He threw the sinker, but it didn't sink. It just floated on in and Mc-Clendon swung and caught it and hit it hard to the right, skipping, skipping, on the ground toward left field, moving for the hole between third and short. Moving fast but not unreachable, not impossible, moving and moving and moving, and there was Christopher sprinting to his right, Manieri to his left, but it went by Manieri and Christopher made the long reach, all this now very slow, very slow, every moment etched in Chapel's eyes: he saw Christopher glove the ball going hard to his right, glove it and start to swing round to throw, and McClendon was not a fast runner, not fast at all, and yet the ball was hit very far before Christopher got there so it was going to be very close . . . and all this took but a long second, two seconds, and seemed eternal and beautiful and unforgettable and magnificent when Christopher fired from a sinking falling dive, fired across the diamond to first base as fast as he had ever thrown, and there at first was a long arm out with the glove open for the ball, reaching, reaching, and McClendon coming, and the ball got there first . . . and the umpire's arm went up . . . and McClendon was there too late, too late, and the game was over and it was done, it was done, and

Chapel closed his eyes to the explosion that came. A moment later he was being carried in the air. Someone pressed a ball into his hand.

The ball.

To the victor . . .

GOIN'
HOME

L ate that night, very close to midnight, Chapel
came back to the hotel. He came back in a car
driven by Joe Birch, and Joe was so drunk he insisted
on driving the car and it was an interesting drive, pos-
sibly the last one of all drives anywhere, up on side-
walks and round and through various shattered places
Chapel could not clearly see, and even when they were
stopped by the police—which happened several times
—that produced another round of congratulations and
some awed faces popping in out of the dark, hands
extended, and the right arm really did hurt, all the way
down to the hand, but it was mainly numbness, not
truly the regal, kingly pain which would be there
soon, very soon, Chapel knew that with certainty, but
had a fine time. Very fine time. The locker room had
been very messy and creamy and madhouse with
noise. All the ballplayers and newspapermen all trying
to take part in "one of the few great moments," and
then the sour moment: the owners came in through
the mess and the crowd; the way was parted for the
holy two, who were carrying much champagne, blab-
bering away messages Chapel could not hear, nor try

to, and putting out hands Chapel was polite enough to shake. Chapel did not want to talk and so did not, and that was easy, but even in that place, among all that foaming noise, they, the owners, could tell from Chapel's eyes that he *knew*, and they did not come within range for long. But they sent in much champagne and so the drinking developed, expanded, blossomed, bloomed, which Chapel did not truly enjoy, because as a pilot he seldom drank at all, but the champagne was *good*. He avoided interviews as best he could. Ross, the TV man, did not show. Chapel knew: he's off already telling the whole story. Well, he's got it, and I guess he deserves it, because if I hadn't known, would I have . . . ?

So. There is a debt. Yes.

One other thing he wanted to do was shake the hands of the men who'd played out there today. He got to most of them. Some of the Yankees showed up, Joe Birch and the last big man, McClendon, and it got entertaining. The moment had come . . . and gone . . . but was locked in there now forever. Much booze, which hit Chapel soon because he was tired, and there was too much in the locker room, too much of being surrounded almost underground, which was not natural to Chapel, who was at home out in the wide free open country and felt claustrophobia coming on. Then there was Gus by his side, at first shook too much by the reality of it to come near Chapel at all, just sat off by himself, starry-eyed, drinking, but he came at last to get the words into Chapel's ear: Ross had broken the news of the trade. Chapel digested.

News story was spreading—flock of those people would be here very soon, coming for the Word. Chapel decided to move on. He grabbed Gus and took him along, making sure not to lose him. Not now.

So out they went with Joe Birch—in the car he'd won as Most Valuable Player somewhere—and some other people, and they went up to Birch's apartment getting happily gleefully almost tearfully stoned and they passed through some of the better times telling the funny stories of this wild thing that happened to Joe, back in the old days, and that one to Billy, back in the old days before "all the shit began to hit the fan," which was a fine old saying from the good old days, and toward the end they were finally beginning to look back on the night just past and see that it was all true, a perfect game, and began to drink to each other as partners in the night together, hard to separate the winners from the losers: it was a day of "Greatness." "One of the great days, Chappie. One of the days of Greatness. Salud." And he drank to Chapel, and after that they quieted a bit and began to feel the emotion of the passing times. Then men put arms around each other—truly an uncommon event, and Chapel couldn't help remembering Carol's question: are you gay, Billy Boy?—and wished she was there. Had she seen it? Did she know anything of it, the—God in heaven!—the perfect game? What would she say now . . . if she knew? I sure hope she knows. I bet she shows tonight. I bet she can't get in. Hell, nobody knows where I am, if she's looking . . . but why should she be looking, stupe? She's gone. Faretheewell, for I must leave thee, do not let the parting grieve thee, for the time has come when even best of friends must part. . . . He started automatically to sing that aloud, and they all joined in and so the night began to end. They began to fade away. Chapel went off thinking about Carol, and then about that last inning, and the whole game was already shaping itself in the back of his head like a great book he'd read and would now be there on the shelf to read always, to move you as the great stuff always did, to turn the pages of innings now and for as long as . . . time went on.

Birch delivered him back to the hotel, along with Gus. Birch hugged him. A dewy moment. They went in the side door and up the back stairs and almost did not make it. They sat together on the stairs and considered each other with deep pity.

Gus: "Poor fella. Bet you're really shot. How do you feel? Listen, I can't carry you, s'help me. I'm smashed. Hit by a shell in the Great War. Can't hardly breathe. But . . . heee." He sat there and began to giggle. Then he began to laugh. He laughed for a long time. Then he finished, wiping tears from his eyes with Kleenex he'd obtained from God knows where, and then helped a stupefied Chapel to his feet and they made it up the stairs to the doorway opening up into Chapel's hall—only safe way to get into Chapel's room without people blocking the way, and it had all been set up for them by the hotel, which had arranged to have the door open and a bellhop there to just see him go by and help him, with gratitude, into his own room. He went into the darkness with Gus and plunked down on the bed. First touch of sadness. The day is done. But, ah . . . this day.

Gus was in a deep chair. He sat there and started to giggle again. Then he guffawed.

"Oh, Christ, I can't stop thinking. . . ."

"What you thinking?"

"All my life . . ." he lifted a fat finger, pointed upward, waggling, "all my bloody life they been tellin' me . . . hee hee . . . they tell me that, quote: *nobody's perfect. Always remember, nobody's perfect.*" He collapsed again, leaned down over the chair, and wheezed. "Gotta tell all the gran'children. Hee. Hell. First, gotta get Grandpa to believe . . . who would have ever thought. . . ." The phone rang. Gus clutched it, said mushily, haughtily: "Whossat? Who? Nah. Absolooly not. Mr. Chapel is at rest and please do not disturb him no more. Got that? No further calls from nobody. Right. Yep. Happy holiday. Same to you. Many of 'em."

He hung up.

There was one soft light in the room, and in the moments to come the peace began to settle through Chapel's mind, the silence to grow, the great wide calmness of a happy, weary man on the edge of the deep and splendid sleep not far off now. They talked a bit, but it faded. Done. Gus, slowly, stood up.

"Well. Billy."

"Yeah. Gus."

"Well. I guess I'll leave you be." Pause. "You need anything?"

"No."

"Okay." Pause. "Jeez, I could sit here all night . . . don't want it to end. You know."

"I know."

"Well, Billy. Mr. Chapel. Sir. I'll be movin on." But he did not move. Then he said: "Billy?"

"Yep."

"Watcha gonna do?"

Chapel said nothing.

Gus: "Shouldn't ask. Couldn't help. But . . . you be here tomorrow? Or . . . you goin' home?"

"I think . . . I'll go home."

Gus nodded. "Figures. No point in all them interviews. Well." He had a small bottle in his hand. He raised it: "Salud," he said.

Chapel moved to the window, looked out at the night sky. No stars visible. Shame.

Gus: "Well. Guess I won't see you for a while."

Chapel turned.

Gus: "No chance I guess . . . to go to New Zealand?"

Chapel: "Never know."

"Yep. Keep the faith. My little Bobbie—you remember the lady . . . she was really lookin' forward. . . ."

"Maybe sometime."

Gus came forward, put out the hand. Chapel took it.

Gus: "Time for me to take off." Pause. "Got to say one thing. Thanks, Billy."

Chapel: "Gus. Thank *you.*"

Gus held the hand.

"Billy? Next year . . . they'll offer the moon. You think you're ever comin' back?"

Chapel moved his left hand up, held the muscle of the right arm. He said: "Gus . . . I don't think there's anything left."

Gus: "Ah. . . ."

"I think it's all gone, Gus. So I think I'm goin' home."

"You give it a rest this winter. And next year, you wait'n see."

"Sure. I'll do that."

"So there's always a chance. I bank on you. Well. Good-bye, Billy. So long. Good night." He went to the door, opened it, stood for a moment in that strong light. Then he said: "God bless" and was gone.

Chapel remained alone in the dark.

Phone would not ring. Instructions below.

So it's done.

The day is done.

Rest now. Think no more.

I can't help it.

Well, go to sleep. Go home. Don't think of her.

I can't help that.

"Billy, you don't need me."

If she saw it, and we were together now, and I could tell her how it was, lie there in bed sharing it with her, all the moments. . . .

Day is not done.

He went back to the window, looked up into the black night for a star.

Must be done.

He went to the phone, dialed Carol's home.

He did not expect an answer. He thought of praying for an answer. Then: her voice:

"Hello."

"Carol. It's me."

"Oh."

"Hope you don't mind."

Silence.

"Won't take a moment. Just wanted to know if you . . . knew what happened today."

"Oh, Billy."

"You know?"

"Yes. I know."

"Well. That's fine."

Her voice was strange. She said: "I heard about it. People were turning TV on so I watched. I saw . . . that ending. Oh, Billy."

"It was. . . . Boy."

"I was. . . . so proud."

"Well. Me, too. I. . . ." Pause.

"I started cheering for you. I wish you'd seen me. Just like high school again. Cheering and screaming. Wish. . . ."

Silence.

Time to talk. He said: "I got something to tell you."

She waited.

Chapel: "You said a funny thing today, in the park, and it kept goin' through my head, through the whole game, while I was pitching. You said I didn't need you."

No answer.

Chapel: "I want you to know . . . honey, I don't expect anything. I'm not asking for anything. I want you to be happy and do what makes you happy. But before you go, I want you to know . . . what I've never said but I've known for . . . a long time." Pause. "I love you."

Long pause. Nothing but silence.

Chapel: "I have for a long time. You're the only girl I ever did . . . fall in love with. I think you're the only one I ever will. You were the best thing that ever. . . . And I will miss . . . but I wanted you to know. Because, boy, I'm in . . . I'm just sitting here in the dark, alone, and I had to tell you. Before I go."

Pause.

Carol: "You're alone in the dark?"

"Yep."

"Me, too."

"You, too?"

"Yep." Pause. "God. It's awful."

"Sure is."

"Billy?"

"Yep."

"Do you need me?"

"Yep."

Pause. "Can you wait a few minutes?"

"Can I wait? I can wait . . . as long. . . ."

"Well, you see . . . it's hard to say . . . must be different (was she crying?) for us old people. But you see, I love you, too, Billy. Oh, God. I'll be there soon as I can."

Phone hung up.

He stood in the exploding dark.

He went to the window.

Now he could begin to see the stars.

Said to himself: know what you did today, Billy? You grew up.

She's coming.

Will she ever leave?

Don't let her. *Love her.*

He looked up, from star to star.

Remembered the prayer in the ninth inning. He put the tired right hand to his forehead, gave an old-fashioned salute, said aloud: "Sir? Thank you."